Contents

Letter		1
	Background	6
	DOJ Has Determined That 19 of 56 Jurisdictions Have Substantially Implemented SORNA; Other Jurisdictions Reported Political Will and Legal Barriers as Challenges	13
	Stakeholders Reported Improvements in Jurisdictions' Ability to Share Information and Monitor Offenders but Had Mixed Views on Effects on Resources and Sex Offenders	23
	Agency Comments	33
Appendix I	Objectives, Scope, and Methodology	35
Appendix II	SORNA Substantial Implementation Checklist Tool	40
Appendix III	Deviations Allowed by the SMART Office in Jurisdictions That Have Substantially Implemented SORNA	42
Appendix IV	SORNA Requirements Met by Nonimplemented Jurisdictions That Submitted Complete Implementation Packages for SMART Office Review	44
Appendix V	Challenges to Implementing SORNA Reported by Survey Respondents from Nonimplemented Jurisdictions	45
Appendix VI	Department of Justice Written Guidance Addressing Challenges with Substantially Implementing SORNA	47
Appendix VII	U. S. Marshals Service Investigations and U.S. Attorneys' Offices Prosecutions of SORNA Violations	48

| Appendix VIII | GAO Contact and Staff Acknowledgments | 50 |

Tables

	Table 1: Key Differences between the Wetterling Act and the Sex Offender Registration and Notification Act	8
	Table 2: Challenges Nonimplemented Jurisdictions Most Frequently Reported with Regard to Substantially Implementing the Sex Offender Registration and Notification Act	19
	Table 3: Selected Stakeholder Perspectives on Effects of Implementing the Sex Offender Registration and Notification Act	26
	Table 4: Titles and Descriptions of the 14 Sections of the Sex Offender Registration and Notification Act Substantial Implementation Checklist Tool and Implementation Reports	40
	Table 5: Department of Justice Written Guidance to Jurisdictions That Addressed Their Specific Challenges in Substantially Implementing the Sex Offender Registration and Notification Act	47

Figures

	Figure 1: Status of Substantial Implementation of the Sex Offender Registration and Notification Act, as of November 2012	14
	Figure 2: Extent to Which 17 Jurisdictions Have Substantially Implemented Sections of the Sex Offender Registration and Notification Act Requirements	17
	Figure 3: Number of Sections of Requirements in Which Substantially Implemented Jurisdictions Have Allowable Deviations	42
	Figure 4: Number of Substantially Implemented Jurisdictions with Allowable Deviations, by Section of Requirements	43
	Figure 5: Number of Sections of Requirements Met by Nonimplemented Jurisdictions That Submitted Complete Implementation Packages for Review, as of December 2012	44
	Figure 6: Number of Survey Respondents from NonImplemented Jurisdictions That Reported Experiencing Major and	

United States Government Accountability Office

Report to the Subcommittee on Crime, Terrorism, and Homeland Security, Committee on the Judiciary, House of Representatives

February 2013

SEX OFFENDER REGISTRATION AND NOTIFICATION ACT

Jurisdictions Face Challenges to Implementing the Act, and Stakeholders Report Positive and Negative Effects

GAO-13-211

Highlights of GAO-13-211, a report to the Subcommittee on Crime, Terrorism, and Homeland Security, Committee on the Judiciary, House of Representatives

February 2013

SEX OFFENDER REGISTRATION AND NOTIFICATION ACT

Jurisdictions Face Challenges to Implementing the Act, and Stakeholders Report Positive and Negative Effects

Why GAO Did This Study

Studies estimate that about 1 in every 5 girls and 1 in every 7 to 10 boys are sexually abused. In 2006, Congress passed SORNA, which introduced new sex offender registration standards for all 50 states, 5 U.S. territories (American Samoa, Guam, the Northern Mariana Islands, Puerto Rico, and the U.S. Virgin Islands), the District of Columbia, and certain Indian tribes. SORNA established the SMART Office to determine if these jurisdictions have "substantially implemented" the law, and to assist them in doing so. The deadline to implement SORNA was July 2009; given that none of the jurisdictions met this deadline, DOJ authorized two 1-year extensions. This report addresses: (1) To what extent has the SMART Office determined that jurisdictions have substantially implemented SORNA, and what challenges, if any, have jurisdictions faced? (2) For jurisdictions that have substantially implemented SORNA, what are the reported effects that the act has had on public safety, criminal justice stakeholders, and registered sex offenders?

GAO analyzed SMART Office implementation status reports from September 2009 through September 2012. To identify any challenges, GAO surveyed officials in the 50 states, 5 U.S. territories, and the District of Columbia; GAO received responses from 93 percent (52 of 56) of them. The survey results can be viewed at GAO-13-234SP. GAO visited or interviewed criminal justice officials in five jurisdictions that have substantially implemented SORNA, chosen to represent a range in the number of registered sex offenders per 100,000 residents. Their perspectives are not generalizable, but provided insights.

View GAO-13-211. For more information, contact Eileen R. Larence at (202) 512-8777 or larencee@gao.gov.

What GAO Found

The Office of Sex Offender Sentencing, Monitoring, Apprehending, Registering, and Tracking (SMART Office) within the Department of Justice (DOJ) has determined that 19 of the 37 jurisdictions that have submitted packages for review have substantially implemented the Sex Offender Registration and Notification Act (SORNA). Although the SMART Office has determined that 17 of the jurisdictions that submitted packages have not yet substantially implemented SORNA, the office concluded that 15 of these 17 jurisdictions have implemented at least half of the SORNA requirements; the office has not yet made a determination for 1 jurisdiction that submitted a package. A majority of nonimplemented jurisdictions reported that generating the political will to incorporate the necessary changes to their state laws and related policies or reconciling legal conflicts are among the greatest challenges to implementation. For example, officials from 27 nonimplemented jurisdictions reported reconciling conflicts between SORNA and state laws—such as which offenses should require registration—as a challenge to implementing SORNA. Officials from 5 of 18 jurisdictions that responded to a survey question asking how DOJ could help address these challenges reported that the SMART Office could provide greater flexibilities; however, SMART Office officials said they have offered as many flexibilities as possible and further changes would take legislative action.

A few studies have been conducted on the effects of certain SORNA requirements on jurisdictions and registered sex offenders, but GAO did not find any that evaluated the effects on public safety following SORNA implementation; stakeholders reported both positive and negative effects as a result of implementing the law. Officials from 4 of 12 implementing jurisdictions who responded to the survey reported that one benefit was improved monitoring of registered sex offenders. Stakeholders also reported that SORNA resulted in enhanced information sharing on registered sex offenders between criminal justice components, in part through the use of certain databases that enable jurisdictions to share information with one another. Stakeholders and survey respondents also identified negative or unintended consequences of implementing SORNA. For example, officials from three of five state agencies and all eight of the local law enforcement agencies GAO interviewed stated that their workload has increased, in part because of the increased frequency at which sex offenders must update their registration information as a result of the act. Officials from a majority of the public defender and probation offices also said that SORNA implementation has made it more difficult for registered sex offenders to obtain housing and employment, which can negatively affect their ability to reintegrate into their communities. The National Institute of Justice (NIJ) is statutorily required to study SORNA's effectiveness in increasing compliance with requirements and the effect of these requirements on increasing public safety. As of December 2012, DOJ had not requested the funding to conduct this study and the funding had not been appropriated. NIJ officials stated that NIJ does not proactively request funding for specific studies, but waits for Congress to decide when to appropriate the funding. Neither DOJ nor the Administrative Office of the United States Courts provided written comments on this report.

_____ United States Government Accountability Office

	Minor Challenges in Efforts to Substantially Implement the Sex Offender Registration and Notification Act	46
Figure 7:	Total Number of Closed U.S. Marshals Service Investigations, Fiscal Years 2007-2011	48
Figure 8:	Total Number of Defendants in Closed Failure-to-Register Cases Prosecuted by U.S. Attorneys' Offices, Fiscal Years 2007-2011	49

Abbreviations

ACLU	American Civil Liberties Union
Byrne JAG	Edward Byrne Memorial Justice Assistance Grant
CURE	Citizens United for Rehabilitation of Errants
DOJ	Department of Justice
FBI	Federal Bureau of Investigation
NCIC	National Crime Information Center
NIJ	National Institute of Justice
NSOPW	Dru Sjodin National Sex Offender Public Website
NSOR	National Sex Offender Registry
OJP	Office of Justice Programs
PROTECT	Prosecutorial Remedies and Other Tools to end the Exploitation of Children Today
SMART Office	Office of Sex Offender Sentencing, Monitoring, Apprehending, Registering, and Tracking
SORNA	Sex Offender Registration and Notification Act
USAO	U.S. Attorneys' Offices

View GAO-13-234SP Key Components

SEX OFFENDER REGISTRATION AND NOTIFICATION ACT: Survey of States and Territories on Implementation of the Act (GAO-13-234SP), an e-supplement to GAO-13-211

This is a work of the U.S. government and is not subject to copyright protection in the United States. The published product may be reproduced and distributed in its entirety without further permission from GAO. However, because this work may contain copyrighted images or other material, permission from the copyright holder may be necessary if you wish to reproduce this material separately.

United States Government Accountability Office
Washington, DC 20548

February 7, 2013

The Honorable F. James Sensenbrenner
Chairman
The Honorable Robert C. Scott
Ranking Member
Subcommittee on Crime, Terrorism, and Homeland Security
Committee on the Judiciary
House of Representatives

Sex offenses are fairly common in the United States and largely go unrecognized and underreported. Studies estimate that about 1 in every 5 girls and 1 in every 7 to 10 boys are sexually abused by the time they reach adulthood, and about 1 in 6 adult women and 1 in 33 adult men experience an attempted or completed sexual assault.[1] In the wake of several tragic attacks in 2005 in which young children were kidnapped, sexually assaulted, and murdered, public and congressional attention became increasingly focused on what was described as the growing epidemic of sexual violence against children. Attention was also focused on the fact that sex offender registration and notification programs in the United States consisted of a combination of 50 individual state registration systems that lacked uniformity and effective operation.[2] Citing a need to address loopholes and deficiencies in individual state registration programs that made it possible for convicted sex offenders to move from one jurisdiction to another and evade registration requirements, in 2006, Congress passed and the President signed the Sex Offender Registration and Notification Act (SORNA) as Title I of the Adam Walsh Child Protection and Safety Act (Adam Walsh Act).[3] SORNA sought to introduce comprehensive standards to make state and territory

---

[1]David Finkelhor, "Current Information on the Scope and Nature of Child Sexual Abuse," Sexual Abuse of Children, vol. 4, no. 2 (1994): 31-53. P. Tjaden and N. Thoennes, Extent, Nature, and Consequences of Rape Victimization: Findings from the National Violence Against Women Survey. Special Report. (Washington, D.C.: U.S. Department of Justice, Office of Justice Programs, National Institute of Justice, 2006).

[2]Sex offender registration programs are systems that law enforcement agencies and other authorities use to maintain and track certain identifying information about convicted sex offenders following their release into the community. Registration also provides the informational base for the other key aspect of these programs—notification—which involves making information about released sex offenders more broadly available to the public.

[3]Pub. L. No. 109-248, 120 Stat. 587 (2006).

sex offender registration systems more uniform, and to create and include tribal sex offender registration systems.

SORNA established the Office of Sex Offender Sentencing, Monitoring, Apprehending, Registering, and Tracking (SMART Office) within the Department of Justice (DOJ) to both assist jurisdictions in implementing the act, such as by providing technical assistance and grant funds, and administer the standards for determining whether jurisdictions have "substantially implemented" the law.[4] The initial deadline for implementation of SORNA was July 2009—3 years after the date of enactment of the Adam Walsh Act. However, given that none of the jurisdictions had substantially implemented SORNA by the original deadline, the Attorney General exercised his authority under SORNA to authorize two 1-year extensions of the deadline to July 2011.[5] For many jurisdictions, complying with the act's guidelines requires significant legislative changes. Some who question the impact of these laws on the criminal justice system and the effectiveness of sex offender registration and notification requirements in increasing public safety have strongly opposed these changes.

Considering the status of implementation and these differing perspectives, you asked us to assess the status of jurisdictions' efforts to implement SORNA and the effect that implementation has had in those jurisdictions that have substantially implemented the law. Specifically, this report addresses the following questions:

- To what extent has the SMART Office determined that jurisdictions have met the requirements for substantial implementation of SORNA, and what challenges, if any, have jurisdictions faced in implementing the act?

---

[4]The term "substantial implementation" is not defined in the Adam Walsh Act. However, SORNA delegated to the Attorney General the authority to determine whether a jurisdiction has failed to substantially implement the act (see 42 U.S.C. §16925). The SORNA National Guidelines for Sex Offender Registration and Notification, issued in July 2008, interpret the "substantial implementation" standard as being satisfied if a jurisdiction implements measures identified in the National Guidelines as sufficient to implement, or "substantially" implement, the SORNA requirements. The National Guidelines further clarify that the SMART Office is responsible for determining whether a jurisdiction has sufficiently implemented measures to have substantially implemented SORNA.

[5]See 42 U.S.C. § 16924(b).

- For jurisdictions that have substantially implemented SORNA, what are the reported effects that the act has had on public safety, criminal justice stakeholders, and registered sex offenders?

For this report, we assessed SORNA implementation efforts for the 50 states, the 5 principal U.S. territories (American Samoa, Guam, the Commonwealth of the Northern Mariana Islands, Puerto Rico, and the U.S. Virgin Islands), and the District of Columbia. We did not include federally recognized Indian tribes eligible under the act's provisions as part of this review because of the unique challenges tribes face in implementing SORNA compared with the states, territories, and the District of Columbia. For example, most tribes did not have a sex offender registry in place prior to SORNA. We plan to analyze implementation efforts for eligible tribal jurisdictions in a separate review and issue the results no later than 2014.

To address the first objective, we analyzed reports that the SMART Office prepared from September 2009 through September 2012 for jurisdictions that submitted packages on their implementation efforts to the office for review. For those jurisdictions that the office determined to have substantially implemented SORNA, we identified areas where the office has allowed for flexibility in meeting the act's requirements. For the remaining jurisdictions, we identified which requirements the office determined these jurisdictions had met and which they had not met. We then analyzed this information to identify any patterns across these requirements. To identify the types and prevalence of any challenges jurisdictions have faced in implementing SORNA, we surveyed jurisdiction officials the SMART Office identified as being responsible for implementing the act in the 50 states, 5 U.S. territories, and the District of Columbia. These officials included representatives of state police departments or attorney general offices. For jurisdictions that have not substantially implemented SORNA, we used the survey to determine to what extent jurisdiction officials are actively working to do so. We also used the survey to identify what actions, if any, jurisdictions are taking or that the federal government could take to address implementation challenges. Additionally, we used the survey to obtain jurisdiction officials' perspectives on the SMART Office's guidance and the criteria it used to determine whether or not a jurisdiction has substantially implemented SORNA. We received responses from 93 percent (52 of 56) of all jurisdictions surveyed, including 100 percent (19 of 19) of jurisdictions that have been determined by the office to have substantially implemented the act and 89 percent (33 of 37) of jurisdictions that have not substantially implemented it.[6] Not all survey respondents provided answers to all survey questions.[7] We also analyzed DOJ reports to Congress on the status of SORNA implementation nationwide and related guidance documents and implementation tools the SMART Office prepared in support of jurisdictions' efforts. These included the National Guidelines and Supplemental Guidelines for Sex Offender Registration and Notification. Furthermore, we interviewed officials from the office to identify and describe the types of assistance provided to jurisdictions in support of implementation and to solicit their perspectives on the issues and challenges jurisdictions in our survey identified.

To address the second objective, we conducted site visits or interviewed officials from a nonprobability sample of five jurisdictions that the SMART Office determined to have substantially implemented SORNA—the Commonwealth of the Northern Mariana Islands, Florida, Louisiana, Maryland, and Ohio. We selected these jurisdictions to represent a range in the number of registered sex offenders per 100,000 residents and the year that the jurisdiction substantially implemented the act. In each jurisdiction, we interviewed officials representing components of the criminal justice system who are involved in implementing or enforcing SORNA requirements. Specifically, at the federal level, we interviewed officials from Federal Probation and Pretrial Services, Federal Public Defenders Offices, U.S. Attorneys' Offices (USAO), and the U.S. Marshals Service. At the state and local levels, we interviewed officials responsible for implementing the act, as well as law enforcement officers, prosecutors, public defenders, and adult and juvenile probation and parole officials. While these officials' perspectives on the effects of SORNA cannot be generalized to all substantially implemented jurisdictions, they provided insights into the effects of the act's implementation.

To supplement information obtained during the site visits, we included questions in our nationwide survey of jurisdiction officials about the types and prevalence of effects observed or expected from implementing

---

[6]We did not receive survey responses from the following jurisdictions: American Samoa, New Hampshire, Oregon, and Washington.

[7]An electronic supplement to this report—GAO-13-234SP (February 2013)—provides survey results.

SORNA and whether they were positive or negative. We also selected relevant national associations and organizations, such as the American Civil Liberties Union and the National Center for Missing and Exploited Children, based on factors such as whether they had testified before Congress on the effects of SORNA. We interviewed representatives from these organizations to obtain their perspectives on the effects of SORNA implementation in various areas. We also sought to identify studies on the effect of the act's requirements in jurisdictions that have implemented the law. Specifically, we searched various databases, reviewed related GAO reports, and corresponded with recognized experts on sex offender registration and notification policies. As a result, we identified five studies that assessed certain aspects of SORNA requirements. We also identified an analysis that evaluated the results of seven studies in selected states on the effect of sex offender registration and notification, in general, on recidivism among sex offenders.[8] We assessed the evaluation methodologies of these studies against generally accepted social science standards and confirmed that the studies' methods were reasonable for our purposes. We also analyzed other documents, such as a U.S. Marshals Service training manual, and data related to federal enforcement of the SORNA requirements. Specifically, we analyzed trends in federal investigations and prosecutions of failure-to-register violations from fiscal years 2007 to 2011. We assessed the reliability of these data by interviewing staff responsible for the data or by reviewing relevant documentation, and determined that these data were sufficiently reliable for the purposes of this report. To the extent relevant data were available from the locations where we conducted our site visits, such as the number of failure-to-register violations or information contained in individual jurisdictions' sex offender registries, we used these data in this report primarily for contextual purposes.

We conducted this performance audit from January 2012 through February 2013 in accordance with generally accepted government auditing standards. Those standards require that we plan and perform the audit to obtain sufficient, appropriate evidence to provide a reasonable basis for our findings and conclusions based on our audit objectives. We believe that the evidence obtained provides a reasonable basis for our

---

[8]Recidivism is the act of relapsing into a problem or criminal behavior during or after receiving sanctions, or while undergoing an intervention because of a previous behavior or crime. In criminal justice settings, recidivism is often measured by criminal acts that result in rearrest, reconviction, or return to prison.

findings and conclusions based on our audit objectives. Appendix I includes more details about our scope and methodology.

Background

Evolution of Sex Offender Registration and Notification Legislation

The practice of requiring criminal offenders to register certain identifying information with law enforcement agencies began in the 1930s in response to the increased mobility of criminals upon their release. At the time, offender registries were viewed primarily as tools for law enforcement personnel, who needed a way of keeping track of high-risk offenders. Registries were generally operated at the local level and primarily targeted gangsters. According to the Vera Institute of Justice, in 1937, Florida enacted the first statewide registration law for certain felons, and in 1947 California passed the first state registration law that focused specifically on sex offenders. By the end of the 1980s, a number of states had enacted sex offender registration laws. In response to a number of high-profile child abductions, sexual assaults, and murders, states have steadily expanded laws to create registration systems that focused specifically on sex offenders since the early 1990s.

In 1994, the federal government responded to the increase in state sex offense registries by enacting the Jacob Wetterling Crimes Against Children and Sexually Violent Offender Registration Act (Wetterling Act).[9] This act provided a national baseline for sex offender registration programs. This affected matters such as defining the offenses that require registration and the duration of registration periods, requiring periodic verification of the registered address, continued registration of sex offenders when they move from one state to another (if the new state had a registration requirement), and community notification. In the years subsequent to the enactment of the Wetterling Act, Congress passed a series of amendments to this federal legislation, which in part reflected and promoted trends and developments in individual states' registration

---

[9] Pub. L. No. 103-322, tit. XVII, subtit. A, 108 Stat. 1796, 2038-42 (1994).

programs.[10] For example, the act was amended in 1996 to provide for the public dissemination of information from states' sex offender registries and in 2003 to require states to maintain websites containing registry information.

SORNA Requirements

Signed into law on July 27, 2006, on the 25th anniversary of the abduction and murder of a 6-year-old boy in Hollywood, Florida, the Adam Walsh Act is intended to protect children from sexual exploitation and violent crime. The act is also intended to prevent child abuse and child pornography, to promote Internet safety, and to honor the memory of Adam Walsh and other child crime victims. The purpose of Title I of the Adam Walsh Act, or SORNA, is to protect the public from sex offenders and those who offend against children by repealing the Wetterling Act standards and establishing in their place a comprehensive set of sex offender registration and notification standards. These standards are designed to address gaps in individual state registration programs resulting from variations across states' laws, policies, and information-sharing and technology systems. These standards encompass the results of prior legislative developments but also extend and supplement them, with the main differences from the Wetterling Act and its subsequent amendments summarized in table 1.

---

[10] Key legislative amendments were enacted by Megan's Law, Pub. L. No. 104-145, 110 Stat. 1345 (1996); the Pam Lychner Sex Offender Tracking and Notification Act of 1996, Pub. L. No. 104-236, 110 Stat. 3093; the Jacob Wetterling Improvements Act, Pub. L. No. 105-119, § 115, 111 Stat. 2440, 2461-67 (1997); Protection of Children from Sexual Predators Act, of 1998, Pub. L. No. 105-314, 112 Stat. 2974; the Campus Sex Crimes Prevention Act, Pub. L. No. 106-386, § 1601, 114 Stat. 1464, 1537-38 (2000); and the Prosecutorial Remedies and Other Tools to end the Exploitation of Children Today (PROTECT) Act, of 2003, Pub. L. No. 108-21, 117 Stat. 650.

Table 1: Key Differences between the Wetterling Act and the Sex Offender Registration and Notification Act

Requirement	Wetterling Act, as amended	SORNA
Covered jurisdictions	• Covered the states, the District of Columbia, and the principal territories	• Expands covered jurisdictions to include federally recognized tribal jurisdictions.[a]
Registerable offenses	• Covered offenses involving adult victims but generally limited to assaults involving sexual acts, such as rape • Covered offenses against child victims that involved sexual acts and sexual contact, but did not include certain other offenses, such as possession of child pornography • Requires juveniles convicted of covered offenses as adults to register	• Expands covered offenses involving adult victims to include crimes for which the elements involve sexual contact, as well as sexual acts. • Expands the covered offenses involving children. • Expands juvenile registration requirements to include juveniles adjudicated delinquent for certain aggravated sex offenses who were 14 or older at the time of the offense.
Classification requirements for sex offenders	• Distinguished between (1) sex offenders subject to lifetime registration, such as recidivists and those convicted of aggravated offenses, and (2) other sex offenders subject to a 10-year minimum registration requirement	• Provides a three-tier gradation based on the convicted sex offense or recidivism: • Tier III: Requires lifetime registration for convicted offenses in the most serious class, such as rape or sexual contact offenses against children under 13. • Tier II: Requires 25-year registration for convicted offenses, including most felonious sexual abuse or sexual exploitation crimes with victims who are minors. • Tier I: Requires 15-year registration for convicted offenses that do not support a higher classification, such as simple possession of child pornography.
Periodic appearance requirement	• At least annual verification of a residence address; did not specify means of verification or require in-person appearances	• Requires in-person appearances (Tier I annually, Tier II semiannually, and Tier III quarterly) at established registration locations to update or verify registration information.
Required registration information	• Required residence address information, with relatively limited requirements for other types of information	• Requires name (including aliases used), residence information, employment and school information, physical description and photograph, criminal history, fingerprints, palm prints, Internet identifiers,[b] and a DNA sample, among other elements.
Sex offender website	• Required the establishment of sex offender websites; left to states' discretion which sex offenders and what information would be posted	• Generally all information, subject to certain statutory exemptions and supplemental guidance, about each offender is to be made available on the Internet.[c] • Includes specifications about search capabilities, such as by ZIP code, and search capabilities needed for participation in the national sex offender website.

Source: GAO analysis of the Wetterling Act, as amended, SORNA, and DOJ SMART Office documents.

[a]Pursuant to §127 of the Adam Walsh Act, designated federally recognized Indian tribes were entitled to elect to become SORNA registration and notification jurisdictions or to delegate the responsibility to the jurisdiction or jurisdictions within which the territory of the tribe is located. See 42 U.S.C. § 16927.
[b]Examples of Internet identifiers are electronic mail addresses, instant message addresses/identifiers, or any other designations or monkers used for self-identification or purposes of routing in Internet communications or postings.
[c]SORNA established statutory exemptions for victim identities, offenders' Social Security numbers, and references to arrests that did not result in convictions. See 42 U.S.C. § 16918(b). In addition, the

Keeping the Internet Devoid of Sexual Predators Act of 2008 exempted offenders' Internet identifiers from disclosure to the public. See 42 U.S.C. § 16915a(c).

Constitutional limits on the power of the federal government may prevent it from actually requiring states to implement specific registration and notification provisions. Instead, SORNA conditions receipt of federal Edward Byrne Memorial Justice Assistance Grant (Byrne JAG) funds on implementation of its requirements.[11] The act initially required that DOJ reduce Byrne JAG funds by 10 percent for those states that failed to substantially implement SORNA standards by July 27, 2009—3 years after the date of enactment of the Adam Walsh Act.[12] SORNA provides that DOJ is to redistribute Byrne JAG funds from nonimplemented jurisdictions to jurisdictions that have substantially implemented the act. It also authorizes nonimplemented jurisdictions to avoid losing 10 percent of their Byrne JAG funds if the jurisdictions agree to reallocate those funds solely for the purpose of working to implement SORNA standards.

Federal Role in Sex Offender Registration and Notification

The SMART Office. In administering the standards set forth in SORNA, the SMART Office is responsible for making determinations on whether covered jurisdictions have substantially implemented the minimum requirements of the law.[13] When making a substantial implementation determination, the office is required to follow the standards set forth (1) in

---

[11]The Byrne JAG Program is the primary provider of federal criminal justice funding to state and local jurisdictions. Established to streamline justice funding and grant administration, the Byrne JAG Program allows states, tribes, and local governments to support a broad range of activities to prevent and control crime based on their own local needs and conditions. Entities can use Byrne JAG funds to support all components of the criminal justice system to improve their effectiveness and efficiency, from multijurisdictional drug and gang task forces to crime prevention and domestic violence programs, courts, corrections, treatment, and justice information-sharing initiatives.

[12]The Attorney General has since exercised his authority under the act to extend this deadline to July 27, 2011, first providing a blanket extension through July 27, 2010, and then granting an additional 1-year extension to jurisdictions upon request. See 42 U.S.C § 16924(b).

[13]The term "substantial implementation" is not defined in the Adam Walsh Act. However, SORNA did delegate to the Attorney General the authority to determine whether a jurisdiction has failed to substantially implement the act (see 42 U.S.C. §16925). The SORNA National Guidelines for Sex Offender Registration and Notification, issued in July 2008, interpret the "substantial implementation" standard as being satisfied if a jurisdiction implements measures identified in the National Guidelines as sufficient to implement, or "substantially" implement, the SORNA requirements. The National Guidelines further clarify that the SMART Office is responsible for determining whether a jurisdiction has sufficiently implemented measures to have substantially implemented SORNA.

the act; (2) in the SORNA National Guidelines for Sex Offender Registration and Notification (National Guidelines), which were issued in July 2008; and (3) in the Supplemental Guidelines for Sex Offender Registration and Notification (Supplemental Guidelines), which were issued in January 2011.[14] These guidelines state that DOJ cannot approve jurisdictions' programs if they substitute a different approach to sex offender registration and notification that does not incorporate SORNA's baseline requirements. Likewise, the SMART Office cannot approve implementation programs if they dispense wholesale with categorical requirements set forth in the act. The substantial implementation standard does allow for some latitude to approve a jurisdiction's implementation efforts. As such, the National Guidelines require the SMART Office to consider, on a case-by-case basis, whether jurisdictions' rules or procedures implement SORNA. Accordingly, for each jurisdiction, the office must assess whether any deviations in a jurisdiction's sex offender registration and notification program from a SORNA requirement will or will not substantially disserve the objectives of the requirement. As a result, according to the SMART Office, it must review each jurisdiction's implementation program, sometimes iteratively.

Each jurisdiction is to submit a comprehensive set of materials (which we refer to as a complete implementation package in this report) so as to allow an assigned SMART Office policy adviser to conduct a substantial implementation review. These materials can include applicable state statutes, codes, administrative policy and procedures manuals, and documentation of database or data-sharing systems and the jurisdiction's public sex offender website. To assist covered jurisdictions, the SMART Office developed the SORNA Substantial Implementation Checklist tool that jurisdictions can use in developing, organizing, and submitting these materials for review. While not intended to be a definitive guide to full implementation requirements, the checklist is organized into 14 sections covering the major requirements of the act, which are described in detail in appendix II.

After reviewing a jurisdiction's substantial implementation package, the SMART Office makes a determination as to whether a jurisdiction has substantially implemented SORNA by taking all of the jurisdiction's efforts into account. The result is a Substantial Implementation Review report,

---

[14]73 Fed. Reg. 38,030, 38,044-70 (July 2, 2008); 76 Fed. Reg. 1630, 1636-39 (Jan. 11, 2011).

which, similar to the checklist tool, is organized into 14 sections.[15] Each report delineates, by section, where a jurisdiction may meet, not meet, or deviate in some way from all of the SORNA requirements. Where the office finds that a jurisdiction has deviated in some way, the determination report states whether that deviation does or does not substantially disserve the purposes of the requirements of that section. For a jurisdiction to have substantially implemented SORNA, the SMART Office must determine that any and all deviations from the requirements in each section do not substantially disserve the purposes of the law, and that a jurisdiction has substantially implemented all 14 sections of requirements as outlined in the checklist tool.

Other federal agencies. The national sex offender registration system is composed of a national database and a national website that compiles information obtained under the registration programs of the states and other jurisdictions and make it readily available to law enforcement or the public on a nationwide basis. The national registry database is called the National Sex Offender Registry (NSOR), which is part of the National Crime Information Center (NCIC), and is operated by the Federal Bureau of Investigation (FBI). The database is accessible to law enforcement but not to the public.[16] The national website is the Office of Justice Programs' (OJP) Dru Sjodin National Sex Offender Public Website (NSOPW), which is an online portal linked to all states' public sex offender registries. Using this website, members of the public can access information on sex offenders in any of the states' individual public registries. State and local authorities that conduct and manage sex offender registration and notification activities are exclusively responsible for the inclusion, accuracy, and integrity of the information in the national registries.

The responsibility for implementing various elements of SORNA is also assigned to other components within DOJ. Under the authority of the Adam Walsh Act, DOJ has designated the U.S. Marshals Service as the lead federal agency in three key missions: to assist state, local, tribal, and

---

[15]If a jurisdiction has a tribe or tribes located within its boundaries that have elected to implement SORNA, the SMART Office also requests that these jurisdictions submit additional information as part of the complete implementation package materials. In these instances, the SMART Office provides a Substantial Implementation Review report that includes an additional section titled "Tribal Considerations."

[16]NCIC is an information system that provides law enforcement agencies with around-the-clock access to federal, state, and local crime data, including criminal record histories and wanted and missing person records.

territorial authorities in the location and apprehension of noncompliant sex offenders; to investigate violations of the criminal provisions of the act; and to identify and locate sex offenders displaced as a result of a major disaster. Under the criminal provisions of the act, USAOs can pursue charges against sex offenders who are not in compliance with registration requirements resulting from prior federal convictions, as well as the law of the District of Columbia, Indian tribal law, or the law of any territory or possession of the United States. In addition, USAOs can pursue federal charges against sex offenders who are not in compliance with registration requirements resulting from state convictions if those offenders travel in interstate or foreign commerce or enter, leave, or reside in Indian country.[17]

---

[17] Pursuant to § 2250 of title 18 of the U.S. Code, someone required to register under SORNA who either (1) travels in interstate or foreign commerce (or enters, leaves, or resides in Indian country) and knowingly fails to register or update a registration as required by SORNA or (2) falls under the SORNA definition of "sex offender" as a result of a conviction under federal law (including the Uniform Code of Military Justice), the law of the District of Columbia, Indian tribal law, or the law of any territory or possession of the United States, and knowingly fails to register or update a registration as required by SORNA can be fined under title 18 or imprisoned for up to 10 years, or both.

DOJ Has Determined That 19 of 56 Jurisdictions Have Substantially Implemented SORNA; Other Jurisdictions Reported Political Will and Legal Barriers as Challenges

DOJ Has Determined That 19 Jurisdictions Have Substantially Implemented SORNA and Another 17 Have Implemented More than Half of the Act's Requirements

As of November 2012, 37 of 56 jurisdictions had submitted complete implementation packages for review, and the SMART Office has determined that 19 of those jurisdictions (16 states and 3 territories) have substantially implemented SORNA and another 17 have not, as shown in figure 1.[18]

---

[18] One jurisdiction, Puerto Rico, had submitted a complete implementation package to the SMART Office for review but a final determination on this jurisdiction had not yet been made as of November 2012.

Figure 1: Status of Substantial Implementation of the Sex Offender Registration and Notification Act, as of November 2012

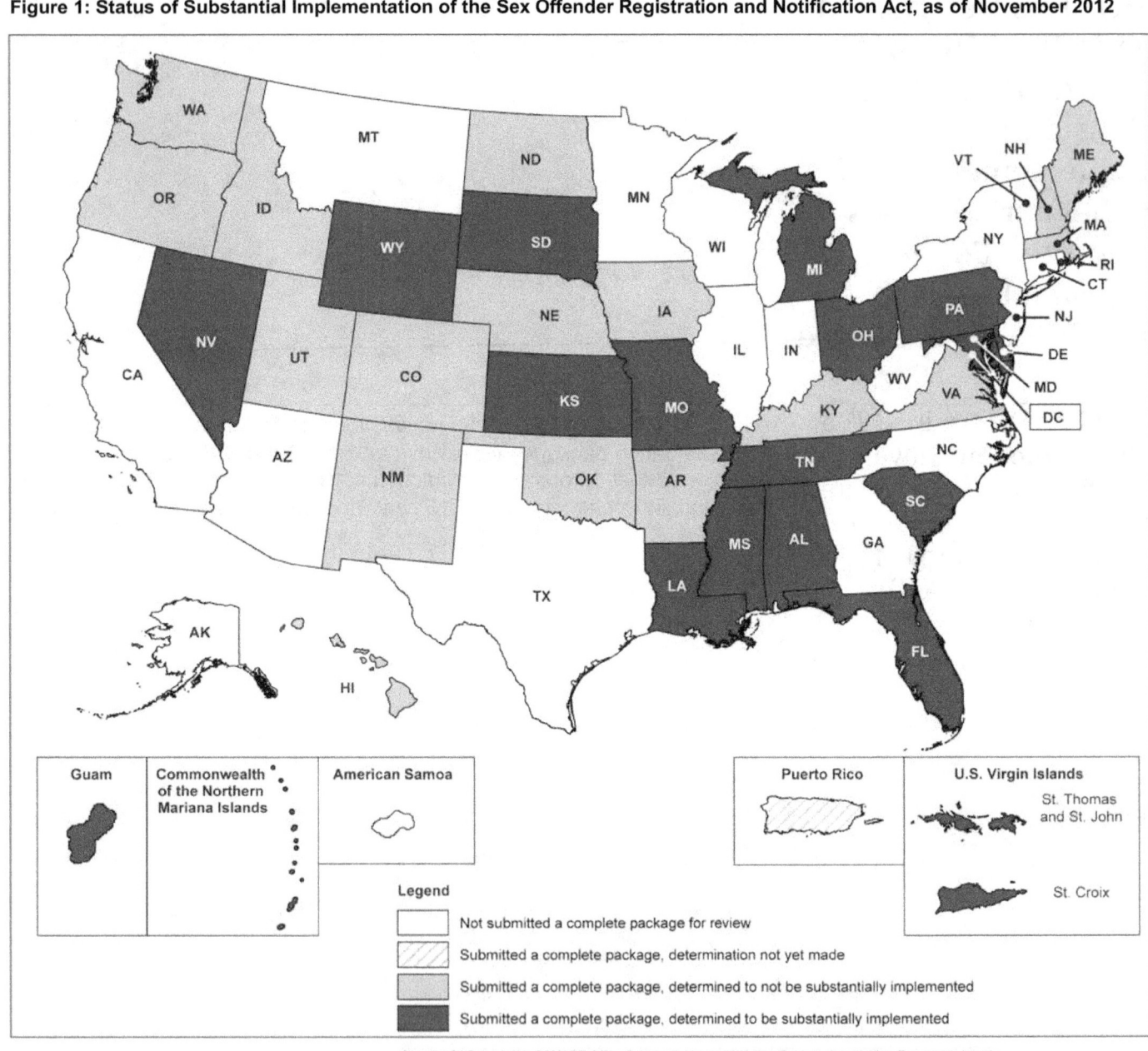

Source: GAO analysis of SMART Office Substantial Implementation Review reports; Map Resources (map).

Note: In administering the standards set forth in SORNA, the SMART Office is responsible for making determinations on whether covered jurisdictions have substantially implemented the minimum requirements of the law. While the term "substantial implementation" is not defined in the Adam Walsh Act, SORNA delegated to the Attorney General the authority to determine whether a jurisdiction has failed to substantially implement the act (see 42 U.S.C. §16925) and the SORNA National Guidelines for Sex Offender Registration and Notification, issued in July 2008, further clarify that the SMART Office is responsible for determining whether a jurisdiction has sufficiently implemented measures to have substantially implemented SORNA. Each jurisdiction is to submit a comprehensive set of materials (which we refer to as a complete implementation package in this report) so as to allow an assigned SMART Office policy adviser to conduct a substantial implementation review. These materials can include applicable state statutes, codes, administrative policy and procedures manuals, and documentation of database or data-sharing systems and the jurisdiction's public sex offender website.

According to the SMART Office, even though these jurisdictions have "substantially implemented" the act, not all of them have "fully implemented" the law given that most of these jurisdictions still deviate from certain requirements—that is, the jurisdiction does not exactly follow the act or the guidelines in all respects. Specifically, 18 of the 19 substantially implemented jurisdictions deviate in some way from SORNA's requirements, including 4 jurisdictions that deviate in 7 or more of the 14 sections of requirements as outlined in the checklist tool. (See app. II for a description of the 14 sections.) According to the office, the substantial implementation standard allows it some latitude to approve a jurisdiction's implementation efforts that deviate from SORNA as long as the deviation does not "substantially disserve," or undermine, the intent of the act's requirement. For example, while one of the substantially implemented jurisdictions does not include employer address, school address, or vehicle information of offenders on its public registry website, as SORNA requires, the jurisdiction does provide the public instructions on its website on how to access this information. The SMART Office determined that this deviation does not substantially disserve the purpose of this requirement of the act. Substantially implemented jurisdictions most frequently deviated from the following requirements: the information offenders must provide at registration, tiering of offenses, retroactive application of the requirements, and offenses that a jurisdiction must include in its sex offender registry. Officials from SMART explained that these requirements, in particular, contain many different components, and as a result, a jurisdiction is unlikely to fully implement all of them. For example, SORNA lists 22 categories of information sex offenders must provide at registration, and many of these categories have subcategories. (See app. III for more information on the deviations the SMART Office allowed for jurisdictions that have substantially implemented SORNA.)

Although the SMART Office determined that the remaining 17 states and territories that submitted complete implementation packages for review have not yet substantially implemented SORNA, the office concluded that 15 of these 17 jurisdictions have implemented at least half of the 14 sections of requirements outlined in the checklist tool. For example, all 17 of these jurisdictions met the sections of SORNA that require jurisdictions to prescribe where a sex offender is required to register (i.e., the jurisdictions in which the sex offender resides, works, and goes to school) and impose a criminal penalty for sex offenders who fail to comply with registration requirements. Conversely, these 17 jurisdictions least frequently met those requirements contained in the following categories related to

- maintaining a public website that provides certain information on sex offenders, such as an offender's employer address or vehicle information (4 jurisdictions met);
- specifying the types of offenses and offenders that must be included in a jurisdiction's sex offender registry, such as both adults and juveniles that have committed certain sex offenses (5 jurisdictions met); and
- specifying that sex offenders must register for certain periods of time and make a certain number of in-person appearances each year at a registering agency based on the tier of the offense for which the person was convicted (8 jurisdictions met).

Figure 2 provides an overview of the extent to which the 17 jurisdictions have implemented the 14 sections of SORNA requirements. (See app. IV for more information on which sections of SORNA requirements these 17 jurisdictions have substantially implemented.)

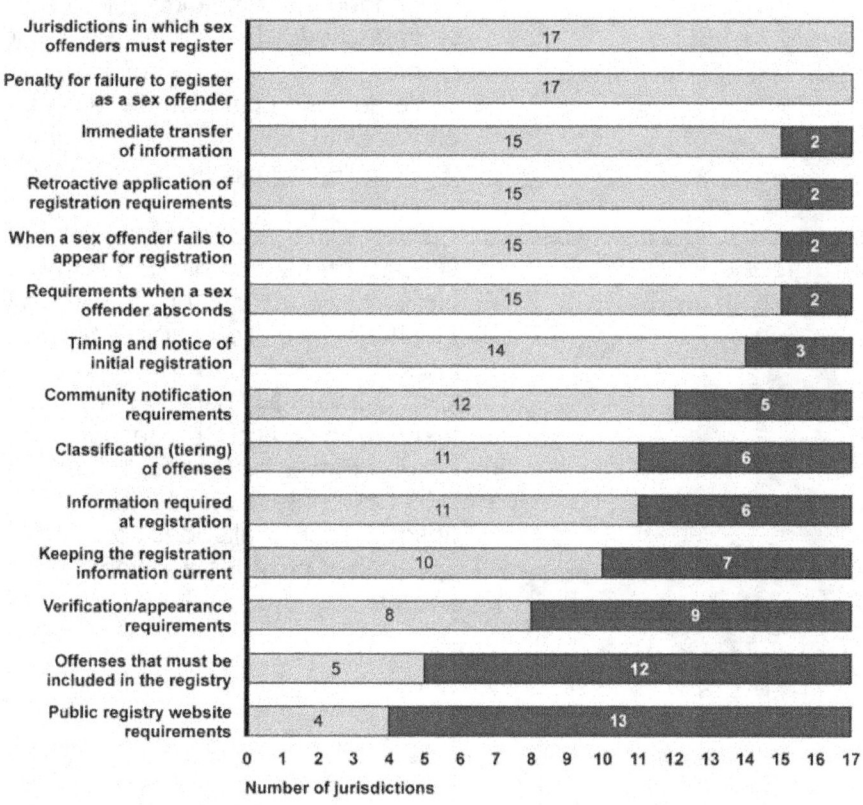

Figure 2: Extent to Which 17 Jurisdictions Have Substantially Implemented Sections of the Sex Offender Registration and Notification Act Requirements

Source: GAO analysis of SMART Office Substantial Implementation Review reports.

Note: These 17 jurisdictions submitted complete implementation packages for review, and the SMART Office determined that they have not yet substantially implemented SORNA.

Officials from 11 of the remaining 19 jurisdictions that have not submitted a complete implementation package for SMART Office review responded to our survey that they are actively working to substantially implement the requirements of SORNA. Officials from 7 of the remaining 8 jurisdictions responded that they are not actively working to substantially implement the act's requirements because of various challenges, which we discuss later in this report.[19] Officials from 2 of the 19 jurisdictions reported that they plan to submit an implementation package to the SMART Office for review in calendar year 2013, and officials from 9 other jurisdictions responded that they did not know when an implementation package may be submitted.[20] For example, an official from 1 of these jurisdictions responded that a time frame has not been set for submitting an implementation package because the staff is engaged in ongoing upgrades to the registration program and has not yet accomplished required legislative changes.

Jurisdictions Reported Several Challenges in Implementing SORNA

Officials from 29 of the 33 nonimplemented jurisdictions that responded to our survey questions on challenges to implementing SORNA reported that their jurisdictions faced challenges. Officials from all but 4 of the 29 jurisdictions stated that these challenges were keeping their jurisdictions from substantially implementing the law.[21] Jurisdictions and DOJ have taken actions, and Congress has considered legislation, to address some or all of these challenges, but jurisdictions identified additional steps that DOJ or Congress could take to help address their challenges. Table 2 describes the challenges these jurisdictions most frequently reported, and appendix V provides additional information on all of the reported challenges.

---

[19] One of the remaining 19 jurisdictions that have not submitted a complete implementation package for SMART Office review, American Samoa, did not submit responses to our survey. According to the SMART Office, however, as of September 2012, American Samoa was in the process of drafting legislation related to implementation of SORNA requirements.

[20] Not all survey respondents provided answers to all survey questions. In addition to American Samoa's not responding to the survey, officials from another 7 jurisdictions were not asked the question about when they planned to submit an implementation package because they had reported that they were not actively working to implement SORNA.

[21] Officials from 29 nonimplemented jurisdictions reported 3 to 13 challenges to their jurisdiction's efforts to substantially implement SORNA. However, the number of challenges reported does not indicate a jurisdiction's progress toward substantial implementation.

Table 2: Challenges Nonimplemented Jurisdictions Most Frequently Reported with Regard to Substantially Implementing the Sex Offender Registration and Notification Act

Reported challenge	Number of survey respondents reporting challenge	Example of challenge from survey respondents
Reconciling conflicts between state laws and SORNA	27 of 30	Under one jurisdiction's current law, juveniles adjudicated delinquent for sex offenses are not subject to registration, whereas SORNA requires registration of juveniles adjudicated delinquent for offenses committed when they were age 14 or older that are at least as severe as aggravated sexual abuse.[a]
Generating the political will to implement the necessary changes	25 of 28	One jurisdiction reported that state policymakers were unwilling to enact legislative changes that would require juveniles adjudicated delinquent for certain sex offenses to register as sex offenders.
Applying the requirements retroactively	24 of 30	One jurisdiction reported that applying SORNA requirements retroactively would increase the number of registered sex offenders in the jurisdiction's registry, which, as of July 2012, is nearly 100,000, and thereby pose a major budgetary challenge for local law enforcement agencies to include these offenders in the registry.
Covering the costs associated with implementation of SORNA	23 of 27	One jurisdiction reported that implementing SORNA would require an investment of an estimated $23.8 million to provide scanners to digitize registry information as well as purchase sex offender registration software for each local jurisdiction. Officials from this jurisdiction also said that ongoing budgetary constraints negatively affected their ability to implement SORNA requirements.
Applying the conviction-based tiering structure	23 of 28	One jurisdiction reported that conviction-based tiering would result in a less accurate depiction of the risk posed by registered sex offenders than the jurisdiction's current practice of tiering offenders based on their risk of reoffending. Consequently, the jurisdiction elected not to implement this requirement or achieve substantial implementation.
Applying the juvenile registration requirements	21 of 30	One jurisdiction reported choosing to not amend its laws to include juvenile registration after a working group found no evidence that the current system in place to address the most serious and violent juvenile sex offenders is not functioning adequately.

Source: GAO analysis of survey responses.

Note: Some jurisdictions either answered "don't know" or did not provide an answer regarding whether they experienced certain challenges; so each item does not total 33.

[a]"Adjudicated delinquent" refers to offenses prosecuted in juvenile court; SORNA requires registration for all juveniles tried and convicted of sex offenses in adult court.

In addition to the challenges they reported above, officials from 22 of the 33 nonimplemented jurisdictions responding to our survey reported that the criteria the SMART Office uses to determine substantial implementation are somewhat or not at all clear, although 6 had submitted packages.[22] Officials from the SMART Office presented reasons why jurisdictions may have responded in this manner. First, jurisdictions may have taken all of the steps toward substantial implementation they can—except for implementing requirements that the jurisdiction fundamentally disagrees with, such as applying the requirements retroactively—and believe that these efforts should be sufficient for substantial implementation. Second, jurisdictions' understanding of substantial implementation is dependent on the extent to which they interact with the SMART Office policy adviser assigned to their jurisdiction; and jurisdictions interact more frequently with the policy adviser once they have submitted a package. Furthermore, to increase jurisdictions' understanding of the substantial implementation process, as of September 2012, the SMART Office posted copies of all the reports for those jurisdictions that substantially implemented SORNA on its website. Senior officials from the SMART Office said this should help other jurisdictions better understand what the office requires for substantial implementation and where it has allowed deviations from the requirements.

Officials who responded to our survey identified actions their jurisdictions were taking to address implementation challenges. The most frequent action officials noted (10) was meeting and collaborating with stakeholders. For example, 1 jurisdiction's senate created a special legislative commission composed of state-level designees from various components of the jurisdiction's criminal justice system to study and report on the legal, fiscal, and policy implications of implementing the SORNA requirements. In addition, officials from 4 nonimplemented jurisdictions reported that they have proposed necessary legislative or policy changes that they believe would enable the jurisdiction to substantially implement the act.

DOJ has also taken steps to address challenges jurisdictions faced in their efforts to substantially implement SORNA, primarily by providing guidance and funding. In particular, senior officials from the SMART Office reported that they communicated to all nonimplemented jurisdictions that they are available to explain the act's requirements to policy stakeholders—and have done so, in person, in 11 jurisdictions—to

---

[22]Officials from 7 jurisdictions stated that the criteria the SMART Office uses to determine substantial implementation were very clear, and officials from 4 jurisdictions stated that they did not know.

aid jurisdictions' efforts to reconcile SORNA and state laws.[23] Specifically, DOJ released National Guidelines in July 2008 and Supplemental Guidelines in January 2011, which were intended to help address challenges with applying the act's requirements retroactively, implementing a conviction-based tiering structure, and implementing the juvenile requirements, among other things. See appendix VI for additional details regarding this guidance.

In addition, in fiscal year 2012, DOJ awarded 11 of the 37 nonimplemented jurisdictions a total of $3.1 million through the Adam Walsh Act Implementation Grant Program to assist jurisdictions with implementing SORNA's requirements.[24] In applying for this grant, nonimplemented jurisdictions most frequently planned to use this funding to acquire information technology, such as electronic sex offender registration software; purchase equipment, such as a system that captures fingerprints, palm prints, and photographs, which SORNA requires; and fund additional personnel. Moreover, the SMART Office received and approved requests from 34 of the 39 nonimplemented jurisdictions as of July 27, 2011, to reallocate the 10 percent of their Byrne JAG funding—funding that they would have otherwise lost—to implement SORNA requirements.[25] For example, jurisdictions could have used this funding to meet costs associated with applying the requirements retroactively.[26]

Jurisdictions identified additional steps that DOJ or Congress could take to help address their challenges. Specifically, 5 of 18 jurisdictions that responded to a survey question asking how DOJ could help address these challenges reported that the SMART Office could provide greater flexibility. For example, one respondent reported that allowing additional flexibility in applying the SORNA requirements retroactively would lessen the jurisdiction's burden with related litigation and operational deficiencies such as hiring additional personnel to register sex offenders convicted prior to SORNA. According to officials from the SMART Office, they have

---

[23] The SMART Office has also provided guidance to jurisdictions on how to address challenges during workshops, video conferences, and teleconferences.

[24] In fiscal year 2012, DOJ also awarded $3.4 million to 12 of the 19 substantially implemented jurisdictions through the Adam Walsh Act Implementation Grant Program.

[25] The SMART Office determined that an additional 2 jurisdictions substantially implemented SORNA between July 27, 2011, and September 2012.

[26] Five of these jurisdictions did not apply for the Byrne JAG reallocation.

offered as many flexibilities to jurisdictions as they can think of within the framework that established SORNA and its guidelines, but they remain open to receiving submissions from jurisdictions proposing alternative methods for meeting the purpose of any particular SORNA requirement. These officials stated that, in their experience, funding the costs associated with retroactive application of SORNA is the true barrier to implementation for many jurisdictions that report challenges with this section of requirements. These officials added that, as new grant funding is made available and Byrne JAG funding is reallocated each year, these jurisdictions should have less of a challenge with applying the SORNA requirements retroactively. Officials stated that for other jurisdictions, however, the retroactive application of SORNA is more of a policy challenge in that some do not agree with that section of requirements and do not want to implement them.

Officials from the SMART Office stated that, despite their efforts, jurisdictions may continue to report the same implementation challenges for several reasons:

1. It may take jurisdictions several legislative sessions to make the many changes necessary to reconcile their laws and SORNA, and legislators may face difficulty keeping the act a priority over that period of time, especially if elected officials who were supportive of the act leave office.
2. Organizations that oppose SORNA have generated political resistance to making the statutory changes to implement the act.
3. The SMART Office is unable to fully meet the financial needs of jurisdictions through the Adam Walsh Act Implementation grant program. For example, of the 66 applications that met the basic minimum requirements for fiscal year 2012 funding under this grant program, the office was able to fund 56 applicants but was not able to fund the remaining 10.

Jurisdictions continue to oppose implementing certain requirements, such as applying the requirements retroactively and the juvenile requirements, because of policy preferences. For example, 15 of 31 nonimplementing jurisdictions that responded to our survey question about aspects of SORNA they would change suggested changing or eliminating specific requirements, such as the requirements to register juveniles as sex offenders (7 jurisdictions), apply the requirements retroactively (6 jurisdictions), and publicly post employer addresses (4 jurisdictions).

Officials from the SMART Office stated that they have addressed all the barriers to implementation that the office currently has the authority to address in the existing legislation and that further changes would take legislative action. These officials stated that they have discussed jurisdictions' challenges and concerns regarding SORNA implementation with congressional staff, and Congress has taken some action. In July 2012, the House of Representatives passed the Adam Walsh Reauthorization Act, which, among other things, would have further reduced the registration period for certain juvenile sex offenders from lifetime to 15 years if a clean record is maintained and exempts jurisdictions from disclosing public information about juvenile sex offenders. After House passage, the bill was referred to the Senate Committee on the Judiciary; the 112th Congress took no further action on reauthorization of the act.

Stakeholders Reported Improvements in Jurisdictions' Ability to Share Information and Monitor Offenders but Had Mixed Views on Effects on Resources and Sex Offenders

Few studies have been conducted on the effects of SORNA implementation on jurisdictions and registered sex offenders. However, criminal justice stakeholders from select jurisdictions we visited reported both positive and negative effects from implementing SORNA. In particular, stakeholders stated that since implementing SORNA, their efforts to track sex offenders have improved through increased information sharing, frequency of registration, and collaboration. On the other hand, stakeholders reported that SORNA's requirement to tier offenders based on the crime for which they were convicted does not consider the offender's risk of reoffending, and that implementation increased workload and caused difficulties in sex offenders' ability to reintegrate into the community. SORNA requires DOJ's National Institute of Justice (NIJ) to conduct a comprehensive study on SORNA's effects, which could help address current research gaps.

Few Studies on the Effects of SORNA

SORNA's purpose is to protect the public from sex offenders and those who offend against children by establishing a comprehensive, national system for the registration of those offenders.[27] However, analysis of the act's effect on public safety has been limited. We found seven studies that assessed aspects of SORNA requirements specifically; however, none of these studies evaluated the effects on public safety following implementation of the act in a jurisdiction. Four of the studies

---

[27] 42 U.S.C § 16901.

prospectively examined the predictive ability of SORNA classification (i.e., the tiering of offenses) to identify high-risk offenders and concluded that the SORNA tiering system was not a good predictor of sex offenders' risk to reoffend.[28] Another study provided a descriptive examination of how the SORNA classification system would affect the distribution of registered sex offenders and associated characteristics across the different tiers.[29] In addition to the results of our search, survey responses also indicate that there are few studies on the effects that SORNA implementation has had on public safety. Specifically, 48 of the 50 officials who responded to the survey question on studies conducted on the effects of SORNA reported that they were not aware of any studies conducted in their jurisdiction.

Although research has not been done specifically on SORNA's effectiveness, research has been done more generally on the effectiveness of sex offender registration and notification laws. Several academic studies have used changes in recidivism as an outcome measure—or metric to describe the intended result of a program or activity—to evaluate these laws.[30] For instance, the findings of a meta-analysis—or statistical analysis of a collection of studies—which analyzed seven studies in selected states that examined the recidivism rates of registered sex offenders released from prison and a comparison group, found no clear effect on recidivism, for either sex offenses or other types

---

[28]Michael F. Caldwell, Michael J. Vitacco, and Mitchell H. Ziemke, "An Examination of SORNA as Applied to Juveniles," *Psychology, Public Policy, and Law,* vol. 14, no. 2 (2008); Ashely B. Batastini et al., "Federal Standards for Community Registration of Juvenile Sex Offenders: An Evaluation of Risk Prediction and Future Implications," *Psychology, Public Policy, and Law,* vol. 17, no. 3 (2011); Naomi J. Freeman and Jeffrey C. Sandler, "The Adam Walsh Act: A False Sense of Security or an Effective Public Policy Initiative?" *Criminal Justice Policy Review,* vol. 21, no. 1 (2010); Kristen M. Zgoba et al., "A Multi-State Recidivism Study Using Static-99R and Static-2002 Risk Scores and Tier Guidelines from the Adam Walsh Act," Research Report Submitted to the National Institute of Justice, (November 2012), accessed December 17, 2012, https://www.ncjrs.gov/pdffiles1/nij/grants/240099.pdf.

[29]Andrew J. Harris, Christopher Lobanov-Rostovsky, and Jill S. Levenson, "Widening the Net: The Effects of Transitioning to the Adam Walsh Act's Federally Mandated Sex Offender Classification System," *Criminal Justice and Behavior,* vol. 37, no. 5 (2010).

[30]Elizabeth K. Drake and Steve Aos, *Does Sex Offender Registration and Notification Reduce Crime? A Systematic Review of the Research Literature* (Olympia, WA: Washington State Institute for Public Policy, 2009).

of crime that sex offenders commit.[31] However, the small number of available studies prevents definitive conclusions.

Stakeholders Reported Both Positive and Negative Effects as a Result of Implementing SORNA

Given the lack of studies and data on the impact of SORNA, as part of our review, we obtained perspectives from representatives of various criminal justice components in five jurisdictions that implemented the act about the outcomes, both positive and negative, that they have experienced as a result of implementation.[32] We also obtained survey responses from state registry officials on the effects of implementing SORNA. The criminal justice components we spoke with included five state registry agencies, eight local law enforcement agencies, six local probation officers, five local prosecutors, and six local public defenders.[33] Some stakeholders, including officials from law enforcement agencies, observed positive effects as a result of SORNA, such as the improved ability to track the whereabouts of sex offenders and to hold sex offenders accountable when they fail to comply with registration requirements. In contrast, some stakeholders, including officials from public defender offices, observed negative effects, such as using limited resources to track sex offenders that are not likely to reoffend and preventing sex offenders from reintegrating into their communities. See table 3 for a summary of stakeholder perspectives. Because of the limited number of jurisdictions we visited and types of agencies that we surveyed, these perspectives provide some insight into the potential positive and negative impacts of SORNA, but do not indicate the extent to which these perspectives are pervasive and warrant subsequent action.

---

[31]One study found increased rates of recidivism, two found decreases in recidivism, and four found no statistically significant differences. The sample of studies included in this analysis was small, and three of these studies had small sample sizes. Recidivism refers to the commission of a subsequent sex offense or other crime. Challenges exist in using recidivism as an outcome measure, however. Specifically, jurisdictions may define recidivism differently or measure recidivism at different intervals, thus preventing comparison of recidivism rates across jurisdictions. For example, in one state we visited, the state corrections agency defined recidivism as returning to prison within 3 years after release, whereas in another state we visited, the corrections agency defined recidivism as violating the terms of probation during a particular year. Additionally, recidivism data captured through the criminal justice system would omit offenses that did not result in an arrest or were not reported to authorities.

[32]We asked about perspectives on the positive and negative effects of SORNA in general, and not every stakeholder we spoke with gave an opinion on all of the themes we identified from these interviews throughout the report.

[33]We also spoke with officials from the U.S. Marshals Service, USAOs, federal public defender offices, and federal probation offices in five federal districts.

Table 3: Selected Stakeholder Perspectives on Effects of Implementing the Sex Offender Registration and Notification Act

Effect	Criminal justice components reporting effect
Perspectives on positive effects:	
Better able to determine the whereabouts of sex offenders as a result of	
Increased information sharing	• 7 of 12 survey respondents from implementing jurisdictions who responded to the question about positive effects of SORNA • Officials from 5 of 8 local law enforcement agencies • Officials from 3 of 6 local probation offices
Increased frequency of registration	• Officials from 4 of 8 local law enforcement agencies
Increased collaboration	• Officials from 8 of 8 local law enforcement agencies
Perspectives on negative effects:	
Conviction-based tiering is not a good indicator of risk of reoffending	• Officials from 4 of 6 local probation offices
Increased workload	• Officials from 3 of 5 state registry agencies • Officials from all 8 local law enforcement agencies • 6 of 11 survey respondents from implementing jurisdictions that responded to the question on negative effects of SORNA • Officials from 4 of 8 local law enforcement agencies
Difficulties in sex offenders' ability to reintegrate into the community	• Officials from 5 of 6 local public defender offices • Officials from 5 of 6 local probation offices • Representatives from the American Civil Liberties Union (ACLU) and the Citizens United for Rehabilitation of Errants (CURE)[a]

Source: GAO analysis of survey responses and interviews with select criminal justice stakeholders.

[a]CURE is an organization that advocates for improvements in the criminal justice system.

Perspectives on Positive Effects of SORNA

Survey results and criminal justice stakeholder perspectives indicate that SORNA requirements have had some positive effects on law enforcement's ability to track registered sex offenders. Officials from 4 of 12 implementing jurisdictions that responded to the question about positive effects of SORNA reported that a benefit of implementing the act was improved monitoring of registered sex offenders, and perspectives from officials representing state registries, law enforcement agencies, and probation offices also indicated that SORNA resulted in benefits associated with tracking sex offenders.[34] In particular, stakeholders identified increased information sharing, as well as other aspects of

---

[34]The other 6 survey respondents did not include information sharing as part of their response. We asked survey respondents about the positive and negative effects of SORNA and identified the most prevalent themes. Not all survey respondents commented on all of the themes identified throughout the report.

SORNA, such as increased frequency of registration, and increased collaboration, as helping them to better track the whereabouts of sex offenders, as described below.

Increased information sharing. Survey respondents and representatives from various criminal justice components said that SORNA has enhanced information sharing on registered sex offenders between criminal justice components, in part through the use of certain databases to exchange information. For example, DOJ developed the SORNA Exchange Portal—which is designed, in part, to allow jurisdictions to electronically exchange information about registered sex offenders. Almost all respondents to our survey question on use of the portal (44 of 50) said that their jurisdiction uses the database. Of these respondents, 34 of 44 found the system to be at least moderately useful.[35] One of the portal's tools is the Offender Relocation Task, which allows jurisdictions to send notifications about registered sex offenders who are relocating from one jurisdiction to another. From January 2011 through September 2012, 32 states and territories used the portal to create 5,422 Offender Relocation Tasks.[36]

Officials from local law enforcement, probation, or the state registry agency in 2 of the 5 jurisdictions we visited also indicated that a public safety benefit of SORNA was that the public has increased access to information on registered sex offenders. For example, one official from a local law enforcement agency said that SORNA has made the public more aware of sex offenders living in the community and has opened up lines of communication between the police and the public on issues related to sex offenses.

While information sharing has improved, local law enforcement, state registry, or probation officials in 4 of the 5 jurisdictions we visited identified additional challenges. For example, officials from two local law enforcement agencies stated that it is still difficult to obtain information from some states on registered sex offenders, such as difficulties in obtaining court documents from other jurisdictions. One of these officials noted that information sharing may be further improved as more states implement SORNA and enforce compliance more consistently.

---

[35]Some survey respondents did not answer these questions.

[36]The SMART Office reported that six states have opted not to use the SORNA Exchange Portal.

Additionally, officials from two local law enforcement agencies stated that sharing could improve if states applied SORNA requirements in a more consistent or standardized way.

Increased frequency of registration. In all 5 jurisdictions that we visited, some sex offenders have to register more frequently as a result of SORNA. For example, in Florida, sexual predators now have to register four times per year instead of two. According to an official from Maryland's state registry agency, approximately 8 percent more sex offenders in the state have lifetime registration requirements and also have to register four times per year instead of two. One official from a sheriff's office stated that the increased frequency of registration gave law enforcement officials a better sense of where sex offenders were supposed to be to help ensure these offenders remain in compliance.

Increased collaboration. Stakeholder perspectives indicate that increased collaboration between criminal justice components, specifically the expanded role of the U.S. Marshals Service, has assisted jurisdictions with enforcing SORNA requirements and holding registered sex offenders accountable for failing to meet requirements. The act contains provisions that expand the role of federal law enforcement, and U.S. Marshals Service officials in all five of the federal districts we visited stated that they have assisted law enforcement agencies with verifying addresses and tracking noncompliant registered sex offenders. From 2006 through 2012, U.S. Marshals Service officials conducted 598 sex offender-specific compliance or enforcement operations nationwide. Three law enforcement officials said that as a result of address verifications and other operations, sex offenders are more aware that local law enforcement is tracking them, which could deter a registered sex offender from reoffending.

In four of five federal districts we visited, the U.S. Marshals Service works with other criminal justice agencies through a regional task force to enforce registration requirements. For example, in one federal district, U.S. Marshals Service officials formed a task force, which is composed of members from the state registry agency, probation officers, and local law enforcement from four localities in the state. The task force's functions include locating offenders who have warrants for their arrest for failure-to-register violations. U.S. Marshals Service's investigations of such violations have increased every year from 340 in 2007 to 3,061 in 2011. (See app. VII for additional details on U.S. Marshals Service's failure-to-register investigations and subsequent prosecutions).

Perspectives on Negative Effects of SORNA

Stakeholders we interviewed, including officials from public defender, probation, law enforcement, and prosecutors' offices, as well as survey respondents, identified the following negative or unintended consequences of implementing SORNA in the jurisdiction.

Lack of consideration of risk of reoffending. Representatives from four of six local probation offices argued that SORNA's classification system inappropriately implies that a sex offender poses more or less of a risk to public safety simply based on the offense for which the sex offender was convicted and does not account for the facts of each individual case when determining registration requirements. For example, a defendant may have committed a sex offense such as rape but pled to a lesser sex offense charge that could result in the defendant being assigned to a tier with less stringent registration requirements than the tier corresponding to the crime the person actually committed. In this instance, the tier is not tied to the actual behavior of the offender, and therefore, is not a reliable indicator of the risk the offender poses to public safety.

Three of six local public defenders stated that since SORNA requirements are not based on a risk assessment, law enforcement resources are not focused on sex offenders who are most likely to reoffend. For example, one public defender said that a client had been convicted of a Tier I offense, but exhibited behavior patterns associated with increased risk of reoffending. However, because judges under SORNA no longer have discretion regarding the tier level of convicted offenders or the frequency or duration of registration, the sex offender remained in Tier I and does not face as stringent registration requirements as those in higher tiers, even though the person may be likely to reoffend.

Increased workload. Some stakeholders reported that their workload has increased since the implementation of SORNA, in part because of responsibilities associated with the tiering of registered sex offenders and increased frequency of registration. Officials from two state registry agencies we spoke with identified the tiering or retiering of registered sex offenders as a reason for a workload increase.[37] For example, one state registry had four out of five staff members in the registry unit devote most of their time to tiering offenders moving to the jurisdiction from another

---

[37] Retiering refers to the process of determining the tier for a registered sex offender that is moving into the jurisdiction to determine his or her registration term and frequency.

state. Such work includes receiving court documents from the original conviction and comparing the elements of the sex offense with the state's statutes so that the agency could determine the appropriate tier for the registered sex offender. For one police department, the increase in the number of times the department had to register or update a registration for a sex offender was greater than the increase in the actual number of sex offenders. This is because the act increased the frequency of registration for many sex offenders from once per year to either two or four times per year, depending on the registered sex offender's tier. Specifically, in 2008, this police department had a total of 4,785 registrations for 2,020 registered sex offenders in the county. In comparison, for the first half of 2012 (as of June), the same police department had 5,694 registrations for 2,079 registered sex offenders. The number of sex offenders increased by about 3 percent, while the number of registrations increased by about 19 percent for this time period.

To help address resource burdens, the SMART Office has offered grant programs and the U.S. Marshals Service has offered personnel, equipment, and funding support. In fiscal year 2012, agencies in 12 of the 19 jurisdictions that have implemented SORNA received Adam Walsh Act Implementation Grant Funds. In most cases, the grantee was the state registry agency. One jurisdiction plans to use the grant funds to hire an additional staff person and fund overtime for officers to maintain all of the required information for the sex offender registry. Another jurisdiction plans to use some of the grant funds for overtime to work with the U.S. Marshals Service to pursue sex offenders who have failed to register. The U.S. Marshals Service helps to address workload and resource needs for local law enforcement by providing manpower, needed equipment, and funds for overtime hours in support of enforcement activities such as address verification operations. For example, from fiscal years 2009 to 2012, the U.S. Marshals Service expended over $6.4 million to help state and local law enforcement agencies conduct 949 sex offender enforcement operations, including over 150,000 completed address verifications, which involved the participation of more than 6,300 U.S. Marshals Service personnel.[38]

---

[38] According to the U.S. Marshals Service, if an individual participated in more than one sex offender enforcement operation, that person would have been counted multiple times: once per operation.

Four of five district or state attorneys' offices and five of six local public defenders offices we spoke with indicated that workload had increased as a result of the implementation of SORNA, in part because the concern about registration requirements has made it more difficult to reach plea agreements in sex offense cases. For example, one senior prosecutor stated that sex offense cases are going to trial more often because people being prosecuted for a sex offense want to avoid registration requirements.

Effect on registered sex offenders. Officials from public defender and probation offices stated that SORNA implementation has made it more difficult for registered sex offenders to obtain housing and employment, which can negatively affect their ability to reintegrate into their communities.[39] While sex offenders were subject to public registration requirements prior to the enactment of SORNA, the act expanded the information required on the registry in some jurisdictions. For example, SORNA requires that sex offenders register their address of residence, employment, and school, and some jurisdictions that implemented the law did not previously collect all of this information. One public defender said that some landlords do not want to rent housing to registered sex offenders because the address of the property would be on the registry. In one state, the agency in charge of the juvenile justice system reported concerns that juvenile registered sex offenders may have difficulties in finding a foster home because of the requirement to register the address of residence.[40] In addition, a senior official from one state's public defender's office observed that since SORNA was implemented in the jurisdiction, the requirement to publish the employer's address resulted in several instances of registered sex offenders losing their jobs.

Public defenders also observed that the complexity of registration requirements results in situations where registered sex offenders are prone to technical violations, and, therefore, subject to failure-to-register

---

[39]This could be of particular concern considering that a report from the Association for the Treatment of Sexual Abusers indicates that factors that may be associated with lower rates of recidivism for sex offenders include social bonds to the community and stable housing and jobs. See Association for the Treatment of Sexual Abusers, *A Reasoned Approach: Reshaping Sex Offender Policy to Prevent Child Sex Abuse,* (Beaverton, OR, 2011).

[40]This agency is currently working with another state agency to provide an alternative address so that foster parents can avoid having their home address on the sex offender registry.

penalties. For example, a public defender in one jurisdiction stated that registered sex offenders are required to appear in person to verify their registration "on or before" a certain date; however, sex offenders must also update their registration anytime there is a change in their information. Therefore, if a registered sex offender had to update that person's registration in between normally required verification times because of a change, such as a new address, that person may not realize that an in-person appearance is still required on the designated verification date. This could result in a failure-to-register violation, which in this particular jurisdiction now has a higher mandatory minimum sentence since the implementation of SORNA.[41] One CURE member who is required to register as a sex offender in a state that has implemented SORNA noted that it is difficult to keep track of all of the registration requirements because they often change, but the people required to register are not always informed of these changes.

A Comprehensive Study by NIJ on SORNA's Effects Should Help Address Research Gaps on the Law's Impact

The Adam Walsh Act requires NIJ, the research and evaluation agency of DOJ, to conduct a comprehensive examination of sex offender issues, including SORNA's effectiveness in increasing compliance with sex offender registration and notification requirements and the effect of sex offender registration and notification requirements on increasing public safety.[42] NIJ was to report its results by July 2011. However, as of November 2012, NIJ had not conducted a study in support of this requirement.[43] NIJ officials stated that the money authorized in support of this study has not been appropriated. The Deputy Director of NIJ stated that NIJ does not proactively request funding that Congress has authorized for specific studies, but typically waits for Congress to decide when to appropriate the funding.[44] If NIJ determines that it does not have the resources to conduct a study on its own, which is the case for the SORNA study, NIJ will competitively award funding to another entity to conduct the study. NIJ officials added that they do not prepare a

---

[41]SORNA requires jurisdictions to provide a criminal penalty that includes a maximum term of imprisonment of greater than 1 year for failing to comply with SORNA requirements. The federal penalty for failure to register is imprisonment for up to 10 years.

[42]Pub. L. No. 109-248, § 634, 120 Stat. 587, 643-44 (2006).

[43]NIJ has funded three studies in support of other reporting requirements in section 637 of the Adam Walsh Act, one of which was a multistate review comparing the SORNA tiering scheme with risk assessment tools.

[44]According to DOJ officials, as of December 2012, the department has not requested that Congress appropriate funding to conduct this study.

solicitation for a congressionally mandated study until they receive funding for the study. However, NIJ may conduct some preliminary work in the area that is the subject of the study to help ensure that the solicitation has enough information so that the applicants understand what is being asked of them. For example, regarding the SORNA study, NIJ and SMART Office officials stated that they have discussed the status of SORNA implementation and potential associated costs.

NIJ officials acknowledged that given the variability in how jurisdictions have implemented SORNA, researchers may face challenges associated with identifying outcome measures for SORNA; determining how best to measure SORNA's impact on public safety, such as whether recidivism is appropriately measured; and ensuring that consistent data are available to measure these outcomes. NIJ expects that the entity that will ultimately be awarded funding to conduct the study would address these challenges when planning and designing the evaluation. A carefully planned, comprehensive study on the effects of SORNA implementation on public safety will help determine whether the requirements of the legislation are achieving their intended effects, or need any revisions, and address research gaps in this area.

Agency Comments

We provided a draft of this report to DOJ and the Administrative Office of the United States Courts (AOUSC) for review and comment. Neither DOJ nor AOUSC provided written comments on the draft report, but both provided technical comments, which we incorporated throughout the report as appropriate.

We are sending copies of this report to the appropriate congressional committees, the Attorney General, the Director of the Administrative Office of the United States Courts, and other interested parties. This report is also available at no charge on GAO's website at http://www.gao.gov.

If you or your staff have any questions, please contact me at (202) 512-8777 or larencee@gao.gov. Contact points for our Offices of Congressional Relations and Public Affairs may be found on the last page of this report. Staff acknowledgments are provided in appendix VIII.

Eileen R. Larence
Director, Homeland Security and Justice Issues

Appendix I: Objectives, Scope, and Methodology

Our objectives for this report were to address the following questions:

- To what extent has the Office of Sex Offender Sentencing, Monitoring, Apprehending, Registering, and Tracking (SMART Office) determined that jurisdictions have met the requirements for substantial implementation of the Sex Offender Registration and Notification Act (SORNA), and what challenges, if any, have jurisdictions faced in implementing the act?
- For jurisdictions that have substantially implemented SORNA, what are the reported effects that the act has had on public safety, criminal justice stakeholders, and registered sex offenders?

For this report, we assessed SORNA implementation efforts for the 50 states, the 5 principal U.S. territories (American Samoa, Guam, the Commonwealth of the Northern Mariana Islands, Puerto Rico, and the U.S. Virgin Islands), and the District of Columbia. We did not include federally recognized Indian tribes eligible under the act's provisions as part of this review because of the unique challenges tribes face in implementing SORNA compared with the states, territories, and the District of Columbia. For example, most tribes did not have a sex offender registry in place prior to SORNA. We plan to analyze implementation efforts for eligible tribal jurisdictions in a separate review and issue the results no later than early 2014.

To address the first objective, we analyzed reports that the SMART Office prepared from September 2009 through September 2012 for jurisdictions that submitted packages on their implementation efforts to the office for review. For those jurisdictions that the office subsequently determined to have substantially implemented SORNA, we identified areas where the office has allowed for flexibility in meeting the act's requirements. For the remaining jurisdictions that the office determined had not substantially implemented SORNA, we identified which requirements the office determined these jurisdictions had met and which they had not met. We then analyzed this information to identify any patterns across these requirements.

To identify the types and prevalence of any challenges jurisdictions have faced in implementing SORNA, we surveyed jurisdiction officials the SMART Office identified as being responsible for implementing the act in the 50 states, 5 U.S. territories, and the District of Columbia. These officials included representatives of state police departments or attorney general offices. For jurisdictions that have not substantially implemented SORNA, we used the survey to determine to what extent jurisdiction officials are actively working to do so and to identify what actions, if any,

Appendix I: Objectives, Scope, and Methodology

they are taking or that the federal government could take to address implementation challenges. Additionally, we used the survey to obtain jurisdiction officials' perspectives on the SMART Office's guidance and the criteria it used to determine whether or not a jurisdiction has substantially implemented SORNA. To develop this survey, we designed draft questionnaires in close collaboration with a GAO social science survey specialist and conducted pretests with 4 jurisdictions to help further refine our questions, develop new questions, clarify any ambiguous portions of the survey, and identify any potentially biased questions. We launched our web-based survey on July 16, 2012, and received all responses by October 22, 2012. Login information for the web-based survey was e-mailed to all participants, and we sent two follow-up e-mail messages to all nonrespondents and contacted the remaining nonrespondents by telephone. We received responses from 93 percent (52 of 56) of all jurisdictions surveyed, including 100 percent (19 of 19) of jurisdictions that have been determined by the SMART Office to have substantially implemented SORNA and 89 percent (33 of 37) of jurisdictions that have not substantially implemented SORNA.[1] Not all survey respondents provided answers to all survey questions.[2]

Because the survey was conducted with all jurisdictions, there are no sampling errors. However, the practical difficulties of conducting any survey may introduce nonsampling errors. For example, differences in how a particular question is interpreted, the sources of information available to respondents, or the types of people who do not respond can introduce unwanted variability into the survey results. We included steps in both the data collection and data analysis stages to minimize such nonsampling errors. We also made multiple contact attempts with nonrespondents during the survey by e-mail and telephone. Since this was a web-based survey, respondents entered their answers directly into the electronic questionnaire, eliminating the need to key data into a database, minimizing error. We examined the survey results and performed computer analyses to identify inconsistencies and other indications of error. A second independent analyst checked the accuracy of all computer analyses.

---

[1] We did not receive survey responses from the following jurisdictions: American Samoa, New Hampshire, Oregon, and Washington.

[2] An electronic supplement to this report—GAO-13-234SP (February 2013)—provides survey results.

Appendix I: Objectives, Scope, and Methodology

We also analyzed Department of Justice (DOJ) reports to Congress on the status of SORNA implementation nationwide and related guidance documents and implementation tools the SMART Office prepared in support of jurisdictions' efforts. These included the National Guidelines and Supplemental Guidelines for Sex Offender Registration and Notification. Furthermore, we interviewed officials from the office to identify and describe the types of assistance provided to jurisdictions in support of implementation and to solicit their perspectives on the issues and challenges jurisdictions in our survey identified.

To address the second objective, we conducted site visits or interviewed officials from a nonprobability sample of 5 jurisdictions that the SMART Office determined to have substantially implemented SORNA—the Commonwealth of the Northern Mariana Islands, Florida, Louisiana, Maryland, and Ohio. We selected these jurisdictions to represent a range in the number of registered sex offenders per 100,000 residents and the year that the jurisdiction substantially implemented the act. In each jurisdiction, we interviewed officials representing components of the criminal justice system who are involved in implementing or enforcing SORNA requirements. Specifically, at the federal level, we interviewed officials from Federal Probation and Pretrial Services, Federal Public Defenders Offices, U.S. Attorneys' Offices (USAO), and the U.S. Marshals Service. At the state and local levels, we interviewed officials responsible for implementing the act, which included five state registry agencies, eight local law enforcement agencies, six local adult and juvenile probation and parole officers, five local prosecutors, and six local public defenders. While these officials' perspectives on the effects of SORNA cannot be generalized to all substantially implemented jurisdictions, they provided insights into the effects of the act's implementation.

To supplement information obtained during the site visits, we included questions in our nationwide survey of jurisdiction officials about the types and prevalence of effects observed or expected from implementing SORNA and whether they were positive or negative. We also interviewed or contacted representatives of relevant national associations and organizations—selected based on factors such as whether they testified before Congress on the effects of SORNA—to obtain their perspectives on the effects of SORNA implementation in various areas. Specifically, we interviewed or contacted the American Civil Liberties Union, Association for the Treatment of Sexual Abusers, Citizens United for Rehabilitation of Errants, National Center for Missing and Exploited

Children, National Crime Victims Law Institute, National Criminal Justice Association, and the National Sheriffs' Association.

We also sought to identify studies on the effect of SORNA requirements in jurisdictions that have implemented the law. Specifically, we conducted searches of various databases, such as CQ Alert, Nexis News Alert, Proquest, PolicyFile, Academic OneFile, FirstSearch Databases, and reviewed related GAO reports. We also corresponded with recognized experts on sex offender registration and notification policies to identify relevant research. From these sources, we identified five studies that assessed certain aspects of SORNA requirements. We also identified an analysis that evaluated the results of seven studies in selected states on the effect of sex offender registration and notification, in general, on recidivism among sex offenders.[3] We initially reviewed the findings of these studies, and a GAO social scientist reviewed the evaluation methodology against generally accepted social science standards and confirmed that the studies' methods were reasonable for our purposes and our reported summary analyses of the research findings were accurate.

We also analyzed documents, such as a U.S. Marshals Service training manual, and data related to federal enforcement of the SORNA requirements. Specifically, we analyzed trends in federal investigations and prosecutions of failure-to-register violations from fiscal years 2007 to 2011. We assessed the reliability of these data by interviewing staff responsible for the data and reviewing relevant documentation. We determined that these data were sufficiently reliable for the purposes of this report. To the extent relevant data were available from the locations where we conducted our site visits, such as the number of failure-to-register violations or information contained in individual jurisdictions' sex offender registries, we used these data in this report primarily for contextual purposes and not as an indicator of public safety outcomes.

We conducted this performance audit from January 2012 through February 2013 in accordance with generally accepted government auditing standards. Those standards require that we plan and perform the

---

[3]Recidivism is the act of relapsing into a problem or criminal behavior during or after receiving sanctions, or while undergoing an intervention because of a previous behavior or crime. In criminal justice settings, recidivism is often measured by criminal acts that result in rearrest, reconviction, or return to prison.

Appendix I: Objectives, Scope, and Methodology

audit to obtain sufficient, appropriate evidence to provide a reasonable basis for our findings and conclusions based on our audit objectives. We believe that the evidence obtained provides a reasonable basis for our findings and conclusions based on our audit objectives.

Appendix II: SORNA Substantial Implementation Checklist Tool

The SMART Office has developed the SORNA Substantial Implementation Checklist tool to be used by jurisdictions in developing, organizing, and submitting a substantial implementation package for review. While not intended to be a definitive guide to SORNA's full implementation requirements, the SORNA Checklist is organized into 14 sections covering the major requirements of the law, as shown in table 4.

Table 4: Titles and Descriptions of the 14 Sections of the Sex Offender Registration and Notification Act Substantial Implementation Checklist Tool and Implementation Reports

Section	Basic tenets of covered requirements
I. Immediate Transfer of Information	• Initial and updated registration information must be immediately sent to other jurisdictions where an offender has to register, to relevant federal law enforcement authorities, and to the jurisdiction's public sex offender website.
II. Offenses That Must Be Included in the Registry	• Certain federal, military, and foreign offenses must be included in a jurisdiction's registration scheme, as well as certain sex offenses for which juveniles were adjudicated as delinquent. • A jurisdiction must capture certain sex offenses, both offenses from its jurisdiction and from other SORNA registration jurisdictions, in its registration scheme.
III. Tiering of Offenses	• Offenses must be classified based on the nature of the offense of conviction, established through a baseline three-tier classification system.
IV. Required Registration Information	• A jurisdiction must collect certain pieces of information from and for each offender that it registers and keep that registration information in a digitized form in its registry.
V. Where Registration Is Required	• A jurisdiction must register an offender if the jurisdiction is the one in which the offender is convicted or incarcerated. In addition, SORNA requires that the jurisdiction register offenders who reside, work, or attend school in the jurisdiction
VI. Initial Registration: Timing and Notice	• When an offender is incarcerated within the jurisdiction, registration must occur before release from imprisonment. • When an offender is sentenced within the jurisdiction, but not incarcerated, registration must occur within 3 business days of sentencing. • When an offender has been convicted, sentenced, or incarcerated in another jurisdiction (including federal or military court), registration must occur within 3 business days of the offender establishing residence, employment, or school attendance within the jurisdiction. • During initial registration, the offender must be informed of his registration duties and acknowledge in writing that he understands those duties.
VII. Initial Registration: Retroactive Classes of Offenders	• A jurisdiction must have a procedure in place to recapture three categories of sex offenders: • those currently incarcerated or under supervision, • those already registered or subject to a preexisting registration requirement, and • those who reenter the jurisdiction's criminal justice system because of a conviction for some other felony crime (whether or not it is a sex offense).

Appendix II: SORNA Substantial Implementation Checklist Tool

Section	Basic tenets of covered requirements
VIII. Keeping the Registration Current	• A registered sex offender must appear in person to update certain changes to required registration information, and must immediately provide changes to other pieces of registration information. • When an offender intends to travel outside the United States, that person must notify the residence jurisdiction at least 21 days in advance. • When a jurisdiction receives notice of an offender's intent to relocate or travel to another country, that jurisdiction must immediately notify any other jurisdiction where the person is required to register, notify the U.S. Marshals, and update the National Sex Offender Registry within the National Crime Information Center.
IX. Verification/Appearance Requirements	• Offenders must register for a duration of time and make in-person appearances at the registering agency based on the tier of the offense of conviction.
X. Registry Website Requirements	• A jurisdiction must maintain a public sex offender registry website and publish certain registration information on that website, such as the offender's name, address information, the sex offense for which the offender is registered, and a current photograph. • Certain information must not be displayed on a jurisdiction's public registry website, such as the offender's Social Security number or the identity of the victim.
XI. Community Notification	• A jurisdiction must disseminate certain initial and updated registration information to (1) particular agencies within the jurisdiction and (2) the community.
XII. Failure to Register as a Sex Offender: State Penalty	• Each jurisdiction, other than a federally recognized Indian tribe, must provide a criminal penalty that includes a maximum term of imprisonment that is greater than 1 year for the failure of a sex offender to comply with its registration requirements.
XIII. When Sex Offender Fails to Appear for Registration	• When a jurisdiction is notified that a sex offender intends to reside, be employed, or attend school in its jurisdiction, and that offender fails to appear for registration as required, the jurisdiction receiving that notice must inform the originating jurisdiction (the jurisdiction that provided the initial notification) that the sex offender failed to appear for registration.
XIV. When a Jurisdiction Has Information That a Sex Offender May Have Absconded	• When a jurisdiction has information that a sex offender may have absconded, the jurisdiction must take certain actions to investigate the absconder and notify various law enforcement agencies.

Source: Department of Justice SMART Office.

Note: If a state has a tribe or tribes located within its boundaries that have elected to implement SORNA, the SMART Office also requests that these states provide additional information, such as an explanation of the working relationship with the relevant SORNA tribe(s), when submitting a substantial implementation package for review.

Appendix III: Deviations Allowed by the SMART Office in Jurisdictions That Have Substantially Implemented SORNA

Nearly all (18 of 19, or 95 percent) of the substantially implemented jurisdictions deviate in some way from the 14 sections of SORNA requirements outlined in the SORNA Implementation Checklist tool, as shown in figure 3.

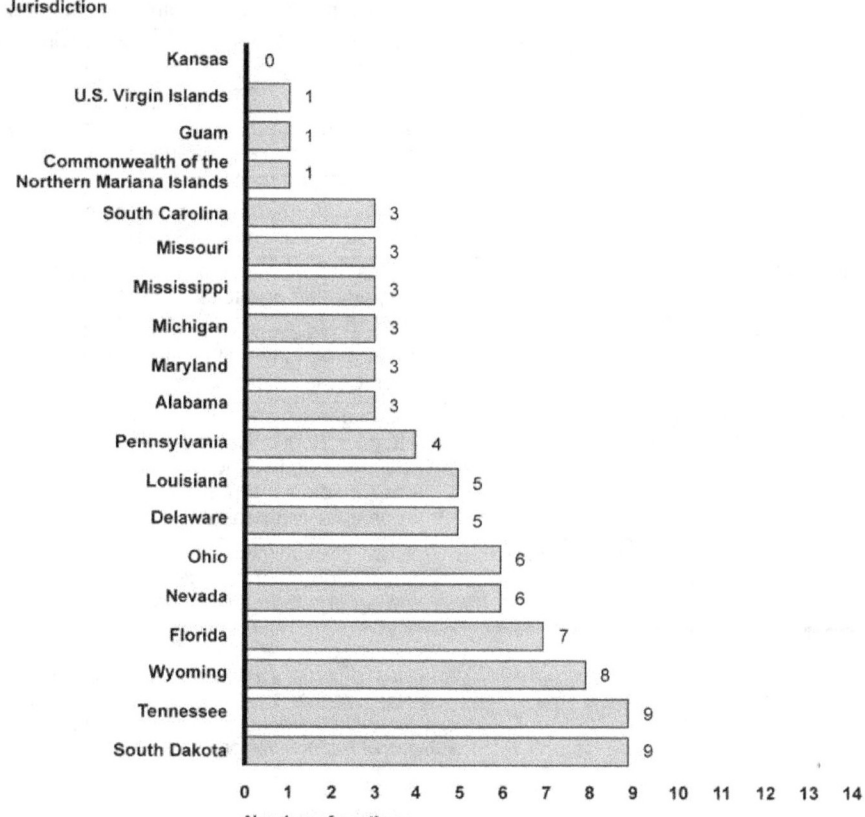

Figure 3: Number of Sections of Requirements in Which Substantially Implemented Jurisdictions Have Allowable Deviations

Source: GAO analysis of SMART Office Substantial Implementation Review reports.

The number of jurisdictions with allowable deviations also varied across the 14 sections of SORNA requirements, with the highest number of deviations being allowed in the information that is required at registration (14 of 19 jurisdictions), the classification or tiering of offenses (13), application of the requirements retroactively (11), and the offenses that must be included in a jurisdiction's sex offender registry (10), as shown in figure 4.

Appendix III: Deviations Allowed by the SMART Office in Jurisdictions That Have Substantially Implemented SORNA

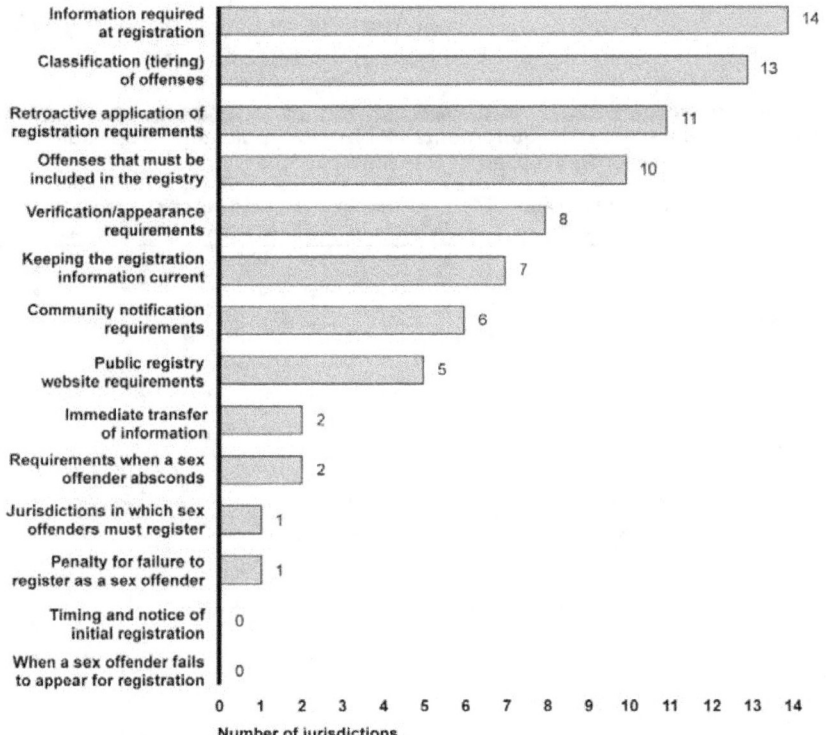

Figure 4: Number of Substantially Implemented Jurisdictions with Allowable Deviations, by Section of Requirements

Source: GAO analysis of SMART Office Substantial Implementation Review reports.

Appendix IV: SORNA Requirements Met by Nonimplemented Jurisdictions That Submitted Complete Implementation Packages for SMART Office Review

The SMART Office determined that, for the 17 states and territories that submitted complete implementation packages for review and were determined to have not yet substantially implemented SORNA, 15 of these jurisdictions have implemented at least half of the 14 sections of requirements outlined in the SORNA Implementation Checklist tool, as shown in figure 5.

Figure 5: Number of Sections of Requirements Met by Nonimplemented Jurisdictions That Submitted Complete Implementation Packages for Review, as of December 2012

Sections of Sex Offender Registration and Notification Act (SORNA) requirements	VA	CO	HI	ID	NH	NE	OK	ME	IA	UT	WA	MA	AR	OR	NM	KY	ND	Total number of jurisditions
I. Immediate transfer of information	✔	✔	✔	✔	✔	✔	✔	✔	✔	✔	✔	✔	✔	✔	✘	✘	✔	15
II. Offenses that must be included in the registry	✘	✔	✘	✔	✘	✘	✘	✘	✔	✘	✔	✘	✘	✔	✘	✘	✘	5
III. Classification (tiering) of offenses	✔	✔	✔	✔	✔	✔	✔	✘	✘	✔	✘	✔	✔	✘	✔	✘	✘	11
IV. Information required at registration	✔	✔	✔	✔	✘	✔	✔	✔	✔	✔	✘	✘	✘	✔	✘	✘	✘	10
V. Jurisdictions in which sex offenders must register	✔	✔	✔	✔	✔	✔	✔	✔	✔	✔	✔	✔	✔	✔	✔	✔	✔	17
VI. Timing and notice of initial registration	✔	✔	✔	✔	✔	✔	✔	✔	✔	✔	✔	✔	✔	✘	✘	✔	✘	14
VII. Retroactive application of requirements	✔	✔	✔	✔	✔	✔	✔	✘	✔	✔	✔	✔	✔	✔	✔	✔	✘	15
VIII. Keeping the registration current	✔	✔	✔	✔	✔	✔	✔	✔	✘	✔	✔	✘	✘	✘	✘	✘	✘	10
IX. Verification and appearance requirements	✔	✔	✔	✘	✔	✔	✔	✔	✘	✘	✘	✘	✘	✘	✔	✘	✘	8
X. Public registry website requirements	✔	✘	✔	✘	✘	✘	✘	✔	✔	✘	✘	✘	✘	✘	✘	✘	✘	4
XI. Community notification requirements	✔	✔	✔	✔	✔	✘	✘	✔	✔	✔	✔	✔	✔	✘	✔	✘	✘	12
XII. Penalty for failure to register as a sex offender	✔	✔	✔	✔	✔	✔	✔	✔	✔	✔	✔	✔	✔	✔	✔	✔	✔	17
XIII. When a sex offender fails to appear for registration	✔	✔	✔	✔	✔	✔	✔	✔	✔	✔	✔	✔	✔	✔	✔	✘	✘	15
XIV. Requirements when a sex offender absconds	✔	✔	✔	✔	✔	✔	✔	✔	✔	✔	✔	✔	✔	✔	✘	✘	✔	15
Total number of sections of SORNA requirements substantially implemented	13	13	13	12	11	11	11	11	11	11	10	9	9	8	7	4	4	

Source: GAO analysis of SMART Office Substantial Implementation Review reports and subsequent determinations reported by SMART Office officials.

Note: A checkmark means that a jurisdiction meets or substantially meets the purpose of the requirements in a section. An X does not necessarily mean that a jurisdiction has taken no steps to implement a SORNA requirement. It could also mean that a jurisdiction has taken steps to address the SORNA section but that the steps taken still substantially disserve the purpose of the requirement. In other instances, an X may mean that, on the basis of a review of the materials provided by a jurisdiction, the SMART Office does not have enough information to determine whether a jurisdiction meets, does not meet, or does not substantially disserve, the purpose of the requirements in a section.

Appendix V: Challenges to Implementing SORNA Reported by Survey Respondents from Nonimplemented Jurisdictions

Officials from 29 of the 33 nonimplemented jurisdictions that responded to our survey questions on challenges to implementing SORNA reported that their jurisdictions faced challenges. Officials from each of the 29 jurisdictions reported 3 to 13 challenges to their jurisdiction's efforts to substantially implement SORNA. Figure 6 displays the challenges these jurisdictions reported.

Appendix V: Challenges to Implementing SORNA Reported by Survey Respondents from Nonimplemented Jurisdictions

Figure 6: Number of Survey Respondents from NonImplemented Jurisdictions That Reported Experiencing Major and Minor Challenges in Efforts to Substantially Implement the Sex Offender Registration and Notification Act

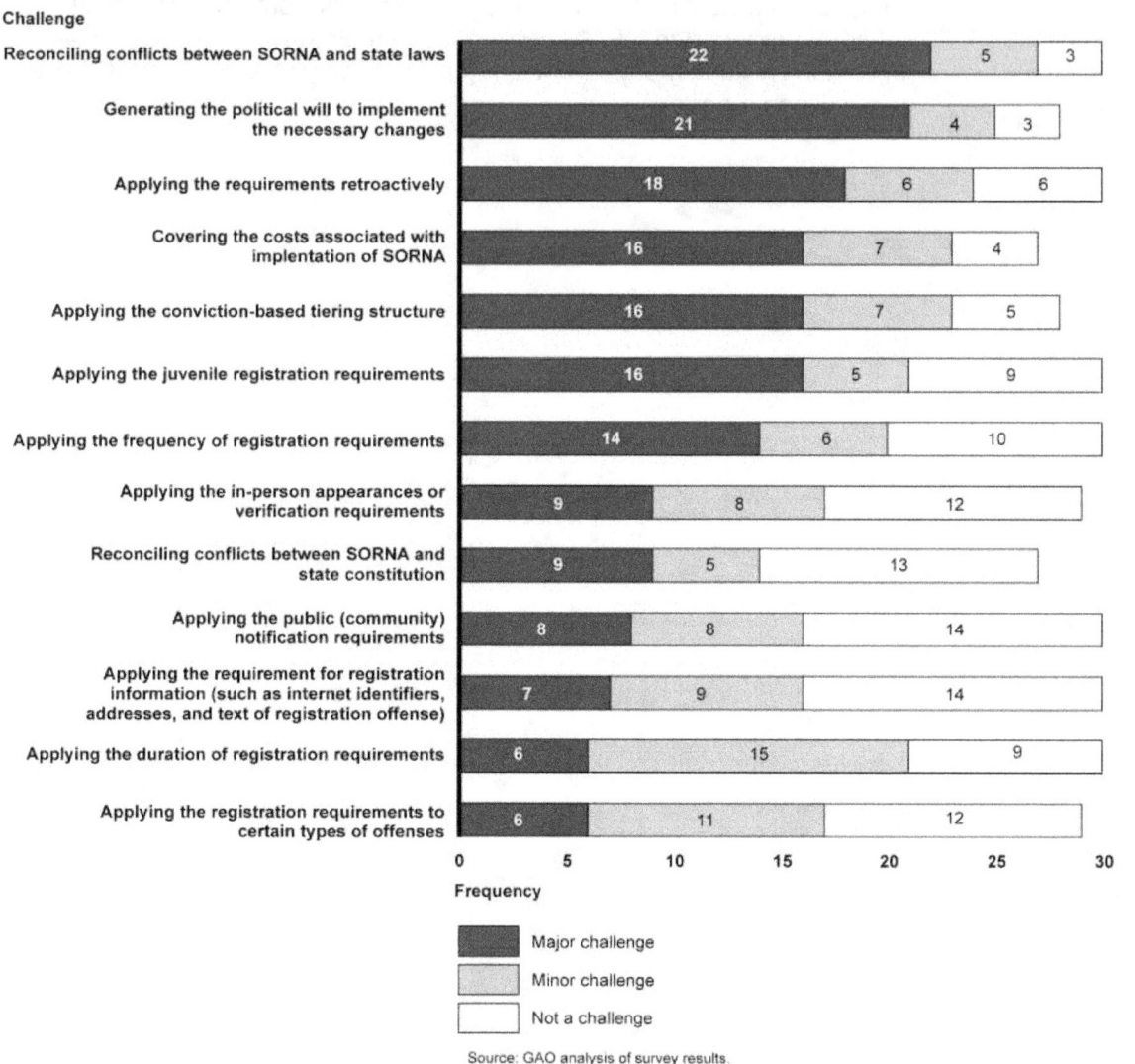

Source: GAO analysis of survey results.

Note: Some jurisdictions answered "don't know" or did not provide an answer as to whether they faced certain challenges, in which case each item does not total 33.

Appendix VI: Department of Justice Written Guidance Addressing Challenges with Substantially Implementing SORNA

DOJ has taken steps to address challenges jurisdictions faced in their efforts to substantially implement SORNA, including providing written guidance. Specifically, DOJ released National Guidelines in July 2008 and Supplemental Guidelines in January 2011, which were intended to help address challenges with applying the act's requirements retroactively, implementing a conviction-based tiering structure, and implementing the juvenile requirements, among other things. Table 5 discusses these efforts.

Table 5: Department of Justice Written Guidance to Jurisdictions That Addressed Their Specific Challenges in Substantially Implementing the Sex Offender Registration and Notification Act

Challenge	Department of Justice guidance
Applying the requirements retroactively	May be limited to sex offenders who remain in the criminal justice system as prisoners, supervisees, or registrants, or reenter the system through subsequent convictions.
	May credit sex offenders who have a pre-SORNA conviction with the time elapsed since release. For example, for a sex offender who was to register as a sex offender for 25 years, in a jurisdiction that implemented SORNA in 2013, if he or she was released in 1994 (19 years ago), then, starting in 2013, he or she would only have to register for an additional 6 years.
	May phase in SORNA registration for offenders convicted of a sex offense prior to SORNA.
	May rely on conventional methods and standards in searching criminal records for details of a pre-SORNA sex offense necessary for registration.
	May further limit requirement to sex offenders who reenter the system through a subsequent criminal conviction that is a non-sex felony offense.
Implementing a conviction-based tiering structure	May utilize assessments based on risk of recidivism as a basis for prescribing registration requirements that exceed the minimum registration period required by SORNA.
	May implement a risk-based—as opposed to conviction-based—tiering structure if the jurisdiction's highest court rules that its constitution does not permit SORNA's registration or notification measures, unless the sex offender satisfies a level of risk that SORNA does not provide for.
Implementing juvenile requirements	May be limited to juveniles at least 14 years old at the time of the offense who are adjudicated delinquent for committing offenses under laws that cover engaging in a sexual act with another by (1) force or the threat of serious violence or (2) rendering unconscious or involuntarily drugging the victim.
	May implement alternative procedures if the jurisdiction's highest court rules that the jurisdiction's constitution does not permit registration or notification requirements for juvenile delinquents.
	May reduce the juvenile's registration period from life to 25 years if certain "clean record" conditions are satisfied, such as absence of an additional sex offense conviction and successful completion of any periods of supervised release, among other things.
	May exempt from public websites and community notifications information concerning sex offenders required to register on the basis of juvenile delinquency adjudications.

Source: GAO analysis of DOJ's National Guidelines and Supplemental Guidelines.

Appendix VII: U. S. Marshals Service Investigations and U.S. Attorneys' Offices Prosecutions of SORNA Violations

As shown in figure 7, data obtained from the U.S. Marshals Service indicate that the number of SORNA-related investigations increased every year from fiscal year 2007 through fiscal year 2011.

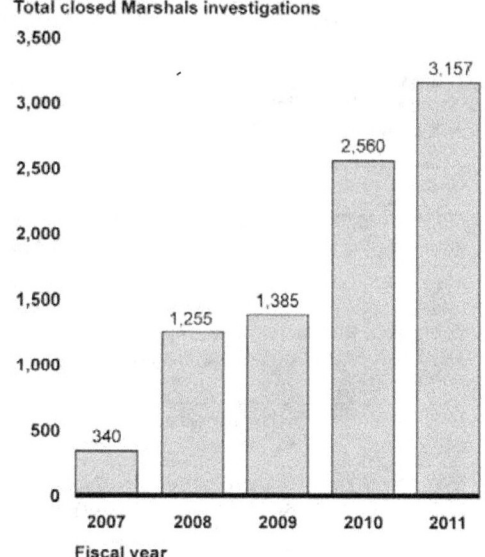

Figure 7: Total Number of Closed U.S. Marshals Service Investigations, Fiscal Years 2007-2011

Source: U.S. Marshals Service.

As shown in figure 8, the number of people federally prosecuted in closed failure-to-register cases by USAOs in all federal districts increased every year from fiscal year 2007 through fiscal year 2011.[1] A majority of the defendants were referred by the U.S. Marshals Service to the USAOs for prosecution.

---

[1] Pursuant to § 2250 of title 18 of the U.S. Code, someone required to register under SORNA who either (1) travels in interstate or foreign commerce (or enters, leaves, or resides in Indian country) and knowingly fails to register or update a registration as required by SORNA or (2) falls under the SORNA definition of "sex offender" as a result of a conviction under federal law (including the Uniform Code of Military Justice), the law of the District of Columbia, Indian tribal law, or the law of any territory or possession of the United States, and knowingly fails to register or update a registration as required by SORNA can be fined under title 18 or imprisoned for up to 10 years, or both.

Appendix VII: U. S. Marshals Service Investigations and U.S. Attorneys' Offices Prosecutions of SORNA Violations

Figure 8: Total Number of Defendants in Closed Failure-to-Register Cases Prosecuted by U.S. Attorneys' Offices, Fiscal Years 2007-2011

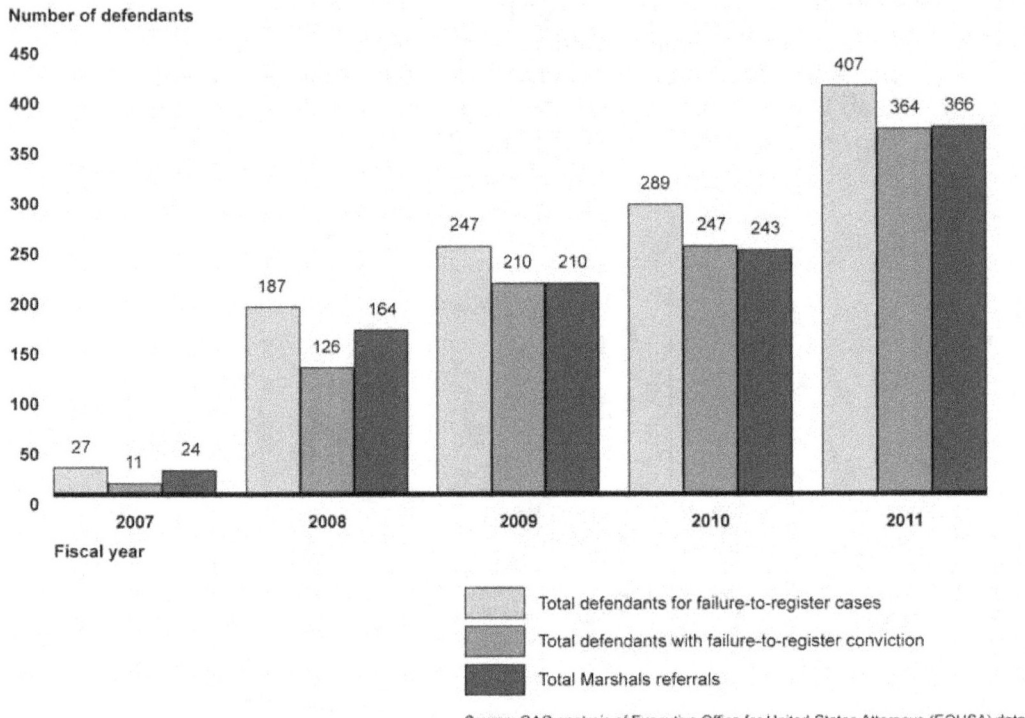

Source: GAO analysis of Executive Office for United States Attorneys (EOUSA) data.

Appendix VIII: GAO Contact and Staff Acknowledgments

GAO Contact	Eileen R. Larence, (202) 512-8777 or larencee@gao.gov
Acknowledgments	In addition to the contact named above, Kristy Brown, Assistant Director, and Hugh Paquette, Analyst-in-Charge, managed this engagement. Alicia Loucks and Amrita Sen made significant contributions to the report. Susan Baker, Frances Cook, Michele Fejfar, Eric Hauswirth, and Lara Miklozek also provided valuable assistance.

GAO's Mission	The Government Accountability Office, the audit, evaluation, and investigative arm of Congress, exists to support Congress in meeting its constitutional responsibilities and to help improve the performance and accountability of the federal government for the American people. GAO examines the use of public funds; evaluates federal programs and policies; and provides analyses, recommendations, and other assistance to help Congress make informed oversight, policy, and funding decisions. GAO's commitment to good government is reflected in its core values of accountability, integrity, and reliability.
Obtaining Copies of GAO Reports and Testimony	The fastest and easiest way to obtain copies of GAO documents at no cost is through GAO's website (http://www.gao.gov). Each weekday afternoon, GAO posts on its website newly released reports, testimony, and correspondence. To have GAO e-mail you a list of newly posted products, go to http://www.gao.gov and select "E-mail Updates."
Order by Phone	The price of each GAO publication reflects GAO's actual cost of production and distribution and depends on the number of pages in the publication and whether the publication is printed in color or black and white. Pricing and ordering information is posted on GAO's website, http://www.gao.gov/ordering.htm. Place orders by calling (202) 512-6000, toll free (866) 801-7077, or TDD (202) 512-2537. Orders may be paid for using American Express, Discover Card, MasterCard, Visa, check, or money order. Call for additional information.
Connect with GAO	Connect with GAO on Facebook, Flickr, Twitter, and YouTube. Subscribe to our RSS Feeds or E-mail Updates. Listen to our Podcasts. Visit GAO on the web at www.gao.gov.
To Report Fraud, Waste, and Abuse in Federal Programs	Contact: Website: http://www.gao.gov/fraudnet/fraudnet.htm E-mail: fraudnet@gao.gov Automated answering system: (800) 424-5454 or (202) 512-7470
Congressional Relations	Katherine Siggerud, Managing Director, siggerudk@gao.gov, (202) 512-4400, U.S. Government Accountability Office, 441 G Street NW, Room 7125, Washington, DC 20548
Public Affairs	Chuck Young, Managing Director, youngc1@gao.gov, (202) 512-4800 U.S. Government Accountability Office, 441 G Street NW, Room 7149 Washington, DC 20548

Please Print on Recycled Paper.

www.ingramcontent.com/pod-product-compliance
Lightning Source LLC
Chambersburg PA
CBHW081902170526
45167CB00007B/3119